RUGBY WAS F★★★ING BETTER WHEN...

A GUIDE TO THE MODERN GAME

PAUL WILLIAMS

First published in 2025 by

POLARIS PUBLISHING LTD
c/o Aberdein Considine
2nd Floor, Elder House
Multrees Walk
Edinburgh
EH1 3DX

www.polarispublishing.com

Text copyright © Paul Williams, 2025

ISBN: 9781915359391
eBook ISBN: 9781915359407

The right of Paul Williams to be identified as the author of this work has been asserted by him in accordance with the Copyright, Designs and Patents Act 1988.

All rights reserved. No part of this publication may be reproduced, stored or transmitted in any form, or by any means electronic, mechanical, photocopying, recording or otherwise, without the express written permission of the publisher.

The views expressed in this book do not necessarily reflect the views, opinions or policies of Polaris Publishing Ltd (Company No. SC401508) (Polaris), nor those of any persons, organisations or commercial partners connected with the same (Connected Persons). Any opinions, advice, statements, services, offers, or other information or content expressed by third parties are not those of Polaris or any Connected Persons but those of the third parties. For the avoidance of doubt, neither Polaris nor any Connected Persons assume any responsibility or duty of care whether contractual, delictual or on any other basis towards any person in respect of any such matter and accept no liability for any loss or damage caused by any such matter in this book.

Every effort has been made to trace copyright holders and obtain their permission for the use of copyright material. The publisher apologises for any errors or omissions and would be grateful if notified of any corrections that should be incorporated in future reprints or editions of this book.

British Library Cataloguing-in-Publication Data
A catalogue record for this book is available on request from the British Library.

Designed and typeset by Polaris Publishing, Edinburgh
Printed in Great Britain by CPI Group (UK) Ltd, Croydon, CR0 4YY

CONTENTS

INTRODUCTION	v
SET-UP	xiii
CORE RUGBY SKILLS	1
PLAYERS	18
SUPPORTERS	45
MEDIA	56
GEOGRAPHY	69
EQUIPMENT	88
OFFICIALS	100
SAFETY	110
MONEY	120
COACHING	130
DIVERSITY	137
MATCHDAY EXPERIENCE	143
CONCLUSION	152

Thanks so much to my beautiful wife and two children,
and my fantastic parents and brother.
Paul x.

INTRODUCTION

According to legend, and a cursory look at Google, rugby was created in 1823(ish). When William Webb Ellis allegedly picked up the ball and ran with it, rugby was born. How true this is, we don't know. But what we can almost guarantee is that no matter how the game started, even after just one day of the sport being invented, some absolute dick will have said that it was better in the old days – even if the old days were technically just 24 hours prior.

As progressive as rugby has become (both on and off the pitch), many feel that rugby 'yesterday' was better than rugby today. But do the stats back this up? Do this author's ill-informed opinions back this up? This book aims to look at various aspects of the game and judge whether rugby's best days are behind, or ahead, of it.

As with the author's previous book, none of this is done as an attack on the game today or yesterday. This author is a rugby nerd of the highest order and doesn't wish to denigrate anyone who plays, officiates or supports the game of rugby in any regard.

Also, it's worth bearing in mind that this book isn't going to deliver a definite conclusion of any note. If you think this is going to be the Domesday Book of rugby and an accurate representation of all that exists in the kingdom of rugby at this moment, or in the past, then you are in for one hell of a shock.

This book is intended to be informative, yet light-hearted. If you believe this book is going to be detailed enough to use in a court of law, or in any educational institution, then you're out of your tiny little mind. Using this book as reference in a court of law will likely end in you doing some serious time in jail. Referencing this book in any academic arena will probably lead to you being kicked off your course (if you're a student) or being sacked (if you're a teacher).

So, with that said . . .

Let the debate commence.

SET-UP

Before we start, we need to define when the 'old days' actually were, in comparison to the 'modern day'. Comparing rugby from last week to rugby in 1890 would be pointless, as the game is totally different – like comparing politics before and after Donald Trump. Also, most of the sources from that period would be written or oral, which isn't ideal. For the purposes of this book, the 'old days' will be pre-1990s(ish). The 'modern day' will be after that period (ish).

You'll notice the word 'ish' is used a lot in this book.

CORE RUGBY SKILLS

SCRUMS

Scrums are rugby's equivalent of the Victorian street urchin who's constantly getting a clip from a 'Peeler'. Whenever there's something wrong with rugby's perceived attractiveness, the scrum gets a quick slap. If anyone ever negatively mentions the amount of ball-in-play-time in a rugby match, scrums get the blame. However, in the 1987 Rugby World Cup there were an average of 32 scrums per game, yet in the 2019 Rugby World Cup the average was just 14 – you weren't expecting that, were you? The completion rate of scrums between both tournaments is also 6 per cent higher in the modern era, with just one extra scrum penalty per match in the modern era – something that flies in the face of what many 'old-school' supporters like to believe.

The fact is that, in the modern era, there are fewer scrums, and they're executed at a more effective completion rate. You could argue, of course, that there are more resets in the modern era. But would that extra time spent on resets equate to the same number required for double the number of scrums? The one piece of data where we can measure the impact of time taken for scrums (and lineouts) is in the ball-in-play time between the old and modern era. In the 1987 Rugby World Cup the ball was in play for an average of 28 minutes-ish, in 2019 it was 31 minutes-ish. The next time that an old man (leaning on the end of the rugby club bar) tells you scrummaging isn't what it was, tell him he's right. It's better now.

Decision – Rugby is better in the f'ing modern day

LINEOUTS

Only someone with a very questionable grasp on reality would argue that lineouts were better in the old days. Without the ability to lift the lineout jumper, which finally happened in the mid-1990s, the lineout was rugby's daddy long legs – in that it didn't look as if it had a fucking clue what was going on and nor did it care. Watching old footage of lineouts is like watching a broken pinball machine that's covered in mud and surgical tape. Made all the more incredible when you consider how many lineouts there used to be in amateur rugby. In the 1987 Rugby World Cup there were an average of 45-ish lineouts with a success rate of 68 per cent-ish. Compared to just 25-ish lineouts in the 2019 Rugby World Cup, with a completion of nearly 90 per cent-ish. It's an incredible difference, until you realise that pre-1970 the situation was even worse. Prior to the early 1970s, teams retained possession from the lineout even if they kicked the ball into touch. It meant that in the 1960s there would be games where there were 110-plus lineouts per match. It was reported that in one Wales vs Scotland game of the period that the centres didn't touch the ball once – literally once. If you know someone who thinks lineouts were better in the old days, you may need to get them medical help.

Decision – Rugby is better in the f'ing modern day

JACKALING

'Jackaling' has probably changed rugby more than any other individual skill within the game. It's the act of parking your body over the ball, after the tackle, and trying to steal the ball from the ball-carrier as they lie on the floor. Reading the above description, you'd be forgiven for thinking that it doesn't sound that dangerous, but it is. There's no other example in daily life where people would be prepared to expose their neck/spine and then let people run full tilt towards it. It is insane. This is an aspect of the game that simply didn't exist in the amateur era. The injuries that occur as a result of players being in the jackal position are the biggest concern in the game and make high tackles look like a cuddle from your mother. Rugby would be a better game without the jackal – of that there is no doubt. The problem is, how do you stop it without bringing back 'old-school rucking'?

Decision – Rugby was better in the f'ing old days

CLEANOUTS

Cleanouts in rucks have never been pretty things. Whether it's 1970 or 2025, if you get cleaned out of a ruck you'll get hurt to one degree or another. But one aspect of the modern cleanout that simply didn't exist in the past is the 'torpedo cleanout' – where players leave their feet entirely and fly into rucks, head-first. In the amateur era, players always remained on their feet, tethered to another play, while in the act of cleaning out. But for some reason that law is no longer enforced. In the modern game you can dive off your feet like some f'ing mental killer whale and fly into the jackaler like they're the actual abusive Florida-based pool trainer who taught you how to do that cruel trick in the first place. Much of rugby's safety procedures are trying to protect players in multiple ways, when one simple solution would often remove a massive amount of the danger – no more diving ruck cleanouts, please.

Decision – Rugby was better in the f'ing old days

DIVING TRIES

Diving tries have always existed in rugby. Very few players have ever been able to resist the urge to score a glamorous try, even though you could snap six vertebrae in doing so. It is, of course, unfair to state that all diving tries are driven by vanity, as many are done out of necessity to score in the corner. But as fine an example as some of those dives in the 1970s were, they're nothing when compared to some of the modern finishes. With a need to keep their feet out of touch and in the air, modern players look like something from the Chinese State Circus – with players often having their feet way above their heads when scoring. If *Britain's Got Talent* ever needs a change of focus and location, send Simon Cowell down to watch some of the finishing in Super Rugby Pacific – it would blow those lip-fillers clean off his face.

Decision – Rugby is better in the f'ing modern day

PASSING

Passing is another one of those skills where trends come and go with each decade, but as a whole the quality has been consistent. Criticism in the modern game tends to focus on the perceived increase in kicking, rather than a decrease in the quality of passing. The major differentiation in passing is arguably within the forwards, especially the tight five. Tight-five forwards are now involved in far more passing scenarios and, in many pod systems, props and locks are key decision-makers. In that regard, modern-day passing gets the nod.

Decision – Rugby is better in the f'ing modern day

TRIES

Tries have changed a lot over the years. You may think that this is merely a comment on the aesthetic of the tries, but it isn't. Tries have changed in value. Tries are the oysters of rugby, initially being worthless, but then becoming a luxury. In the 1880s in London, oysters were largely worthless and considered a peasant food. Rugby tries have followed a similar path. In the 1880s they were worth nothing and simply gave you a 'try' to kick at goal. That has, of course, changed over the years, with their value increasing from one to five points over the past 140 years.

However, while their numeric value is clear and objective, their value aesthetically from the amateur era to the pro era is a subject of contention. According to most men over 70, rugby players used to score tries that were more akin to art than sport. Ask any supporters about the type of tries that were scored from the 1970s through to the mid-1990s and you'd swear that you were listening to a review of the Vaganova Ballet Academy in St Petersburg. Also, back in the day, according to the sages from yesteryear, many more tries were scored. But the data doesn't back it up. In the 1987 Rugby World Cup, for example, there was an average of seven-ish tries scored per game. In the 2019 World Cup there were 6.25-ish tries scored per game. The debate should really focus not on the number of tries scored, but the defence systems that they were scored against. Scoring a try in the 1970s was far easier than scoring a try in 2025. It just was. This won't be popular, but tries in the modern age are far harder to score and therefore better by definition.

Decision – Rugby is better in the f'ing modern day

KICKING FROM HAND

Talk to anyone about the modern game and they'll mention that players now kick the ball too much – that seems to be most supporters' gripe. But while many fans still want players to run blindly with the ball (into three-man tackles) and risk getting turned into human Ardennes paté – most coaches don't. Modern rugby requires more kicking not because players and coaches love kicking, but because there's simply less space than there was in the past – modern rugby is like flying Ryanair. But more than that, there's some data to suggest that modern rugby actually kicks less. In the 2023 Rugby World Cup, for instance, teams kicked about 25–30 per cent-ish less per minute than in 1987. Another weird stat that may blow your mind with regards to kicking is that the highest total number of kicks in a match at the 2023 World Cup was 82-ish. With England kicking more than any other team in that competition with 33.8-ish kicks per match. Compare to that to the 106 total in the 1973 Barbarians vs New Zealand match. If you split that number down the middle, for mathematical simplicity, it means that on average the 'best match of all time' had two teams kick over 50 times each, in 80 minutes. If you're over a certain age this stat will have just made you angry and have you reaching for a pint of mild ale.

Decision – The author of this book can't f'ing decide

TYPES OF KICK

While the data around kicking frequency suggests that modern rugby kicks largely the same amount of ball as they did in the past, maybe less, the type of kicking has changed. Box-kicks, for instance, now make up about 25 per cent-ish of all kicks taken, whereas in 1987 it was about 5 per cent-ish. Box-kicks are, of course, a necessary part of rugby/life, but so are those plastic boxes from Ikea that seem to collect in your house and turn your life into a shit game of Tetris. So, Ikea boxes and box-kicks can both f'off.

Decision – Rugby was better in the f'ing old days

THE SPIRAL-KICK

The spiral-kick was once the only kick in town – especially in the 80s and 90s. Being able to spiral-kick a rugby ball was a rite of passage. It was like being able to drive a car or use the 'nudges' properly on a gambling machine. However, the spiral-kick was a cruel bastard. Much like tight jeans, it looked cool but caused problems with your balls. A spiral-kick either flew through the air like something NASA would be proud to produce or flew immediately off the side of your foot and into the car park like a pissed-up pigeon. As an aside, with the number of pigeons/seagulls that the author of this book has seen drinking directly from pints of lager/cider, it's amazing that they don't fight more on the streets – but it does also explain why they're drawn increasingly to chips and kebabs.

We digress. With the spiral-kick becoming an ever-riskier option, the 'end-on-end kick' came into fashion

– it meant less distance, but also less risk. In recent seasons we've seen the spiral-kick return. Especially the 'spiral bomb', which involves sending a spiral-kick up into the air with a spiral so tight that what goes up as a normal rugby ball comes down with the same force and velocity as some kind of new metal-based weapon invented by the Russians.

Decision – Rugby was better in the f'ing old days (bring back more spiral-kicks)

GOAL-KICKING

Goal-kicking is the gold of rugby, in that its value hasn't really changed and it remains the most precious commodity in rugby. Yes, we now have the deadly 'driving maul', which you could argue is the diamond/platinum of rugby, but goal-kicking is still where it's at. No one remembers their team not winning a match because they missed a try-scoring opportunity, but everyone remembers when they lost because they missed a kick at goal. Data on the change in goal-kicking accuracy over the years is scant. While every other inch of the game seems to have been analysed to death, the comparison between goal-kicking in the old day to the modern days is somewhat absent. One thing we can agree on is that the shape/ball-flight of goal-kicking has certainly changed. In the amateur era, the ball tended to have a massive arc from the right to left (a hook, if it was a right-footed kicker), whereas in the modern day the kicking arc is far straighter, almost a slice (if a right-footed kicker). Most of this difference in ball flight is due to the difference in the equipment used and the stance of the kicker. Before the pro era, goal-kickers placed the ball on mud or sand, which seems incredibly old-fashioned now – almost medieval. If you took a load of schoolkids on a rugby history tour and showed them a mud-based kicking tee in 2025, they'd assume it was Henry VIII's. As a brief historical aside, Henry VIII was actually called that because he played first-five-eighth in school, not because he was the eighth Henry to be crowned King of England. Some of those who don't trust 'mainstream media' and 'mainstream history' remain adamant that it was because he played number eight at school, but there is little evidence to back this up. There's a similar lack of evidence for the theory that he killed or divorced six wives because he hated blindside flankers and the number that they wear on their backs.

We digress, again. The stance of kickers also radically shaped the way that goal kicks move in the air. In the amateur era, most goal-kickers approached from a side angle, like a shady bloke selling illegal hotdogs on London's Oxford Street. Now the approach is far straighter, more head-on, more like ordering food from Five Guys. The quality of goal-kicking is arguably better now than it has ever been, especially when it comes to distance. But you could argue that the improvements are the direct result of the equipment use.

Decision – It's a f'ing draw, the author can't decide

DROP-GOALS

The drop-goal is the long-lost friend of rugby. That pal who you were very friendly with in the 1980s and 1990s and then sadly drifted apart – it's essentially my Carl Bushell (if you read this, Carl, I hope you're keeping okay). With the increased consistency in lineout techniques and the use of attacking mauls in the attacking 22m area, the drop-goal has largely been banished. Once the deadly finishing move that wouldn't look out of place in Tekken, it has become rather a quaint, atavistic act that now sits gathering dust on rugby's kicking shelf. But for the purists out there, the drop-goal remains a remarkable sight. It's the most difficult kick in the game. Using a ball that's about as trustworthy as a Reform Party leader on the piss in Vegas and then having to drop it from about two and half feet, on to a surface that has essentially had human cattle running around on it for 70 minutes, is a recipe for disaster.

The drop-goal remains one of the few skills in rugby that can still make even the best players in the world look like they've never kicked a ball before, ever. You could have a six-Test-cap British and Irish Lions outside-half attempt a drop-goal and it still has only a 50 per cent chance of having the same trajectory as if your nan has had a pop from 20 metres. It's also arguable that the speed and fitness of modern pros, along with eight-player benches, has made drop-goals far harder from a 'defensive blocking' standpoint. In the amateur era, the final few minutes meant you had a lot of tired players on the pitch, less likely to get off the line quickly enough to pressure the kicker, but now you have at least seven players charging the kicker like they're Ben Johnson in 1988. Despite the difficulty and low ratio access, drop-goals are beautiful. Proper beautiful.

Decision – Rugby was better in the f'ing old days

DEFENCE

You could argue that defensive systems in modern rugby have changed the game more than any other single aspect of the sport. With the game having gone pro and the increasing influence of rugby league in union's defensive plans, the pitch became a lot smaller. Whereas players in the 1970s, 80s and 90s were largely running into one tackler and a defensive structure that merely meant 'numbering up' with the player opposite, the pro game brought with it a far more complicated scenario for attackers. Where you once just had to focus on the player in front of you, now you had to worry about 'blitz' defences, 'drift' defences and more recently 'hybrid' defence. The result was that a once rather static defensive picture had now turned into the type of dynamic image that air-traffic controllers tend to see over Heathrow Airport. With fitter and faster players, the modern outside-half now doesn't just have to beat the opposition 10, they have to beat the 10, 12 and often two back-row forwards – which is regularly cited as the major reason for the demise of the purely creative outside-half.

Since the game turned pro, defensive stats have gone through the roof. A great example comes from the difference between tackle stats in the 1987 Rugby

World Cup and that in 2019. In 1987, the average team made tackles in the range of 48-ish per match, with a tackle completion of just 70 per cent-ish. In 2019, teams made an average of 130-ish with a completion percentage of 84 per cent-ish. While the greater efficiency of defences has obviously improved hugely over the years and the game is far better in that regard, it hasn't necessarily translated into making it a better spectacle. Missed tackles are what makes rugby, rugby. Without missed tackles there are very few line breaks and very few tries. You could argue that we need more missed tackles, not fewer.

Decision – Rugby was better in the f'ing old days

TAKING THE HIGH BALL

Taking a high ball has always required a level of bravery not usually seen outside of the military. There are marines who would think twice about catching a spiral bomb with three back-row forwards running at them – many of whom will have experience with real bombs. But back in the amateur days, the catching of a high ball was far more dangerous. In the modern day, catching a high ball still means dealing with a few dangerous people running at the catcher, but back in the amateur days it was like having serial killers coming for you. In the modern day you have to wait for the player to land and be aware of all the players and dynamics happening around you. In 1970, you could essentially swing a flesh axe at the catcher's head and worry about little else.

Decision – Catching a high ball has always required a lot of f'ing bottle

PLAYERS

PLAYER SIZE

Before we mention players and their specific positions, the overall physical shape of rugby players has changed dramatically from the old to the modern period – and ridiculously so. Players in the 1970s, 1980s and 1990s were more 'slim-fit' – in that they could all easily fit into a slim-fit shirt from an Italian/Spanish clothing designer; think Zara or Dolce & Gabbana, for instance. Cut to a player from the past 20 years and a modern player would look like a Steiff Teddy Bear in a 'slim-fit' shirt.

To use a less obtuse example, since the game turned professional, rugby players are on average four inches taller and 14kg heavier – that's two stones and two pounds. That's a lot. Hell of a lot. Whether you think the game was a better spectacle with smaller players is up for debate. What isn't up for debate is that the size, speed and agility of modern players is far greater than their predecessors. Tackling a player in the 1970s was like tackling a normal man on the street. Tackling a player in the modern game is like tackling that street, if it was uprooted and thrown at your chest. Modern players are bigger and faster than they have ever been – there is no argument. If you don't think a modern player is faster, bigger, stronger and harder to tackle than a player from the 1970s and 1980s, then one can presume that you stopped watching rugby during that period. There are plenty of people like that about. They'll confidently tell you rugby was better in the 1970s, then admit they don't watch the game now. It's like telling foodies in 2025 that cold prawns, peas and cheese, served in a light green gelatine mould, is the best food ever – even though they haven't tasted anything else since 1973. Why were people in the 1970s so obsessed with food in gelatine?

Decision – Rugby is better in the f'ing modern day

JONAH LOMU, WE OWE IT ALL TO HIM

Apologies for the slight delay in discussing the specifics of players and their positions. But we cannot truly appreciate the differences between modern and old-school players, without mentioning Jonah Lomu. He was the line in the sand. The massive 6ft 5in, 19 stone, 11 seconds over 100 metres line in the f'ing sand. It's no oversimplification to say that there was rugby before Jonah Lomu and after him. Without wishing to offend any religious denominations, it's like the whole BC/AD thing. In rugby, there's BL and AL. There had been destructive 'bigger' players in the years previous to Lomu, but nothing quite like him. It was like having access to nuclear weapons during the Norman invasion of England. Lomu ran through the wall that was amateur rugby, and when he crashed through to the other side, professional rugby was born. RIP, Jonah – unplayable.

Decision – Rugby is better in the f'ing modern day

TIGHTHEAD

Tighthead in rugby is a position that has changed a great deal, while seemingly having changed little. The core role of a tighthead is to scrummage, and it always has been. Rugby players are often rather neatly split into two categories – piano players (the backs), and piano movers (the forwards). But tightheads deserve a piano-related tag of their own; they are the piano – massive f'ing grand pianos – if that piano had stubble and could easily eat three Big Mac meals and 20 nuggets. Whether you played in 1980 or are playing in 2025, the scrummage remains one of the key parts of rugby – especially at Test level. If your team doesn't have a decent tighthead, you'll witness more collapses than Liz Truss.

While the scrummaging requirement of a tighthead has changed little, the fitness required of tightheads has changed enormously. Whereas tightheads used to be able to scrummage and then down tools like a print worker in the 1980s, they're now required to hit far more rucks, make more tackles and perform a bigger role with the ball. Tighthead props now play a massive role in modern pod systems. And while their role is rarely to carry the ball, their need to hit that next ruck is crucial. The result is that tighthead props now look more like looseheads – and due to similar fitness requirements, modern looseheads that look more like hookers.

In the modern game, the tighthead (especially at elite level) has become a rare beast. You need only look at the top earners by position in professional rugby to realise how important tightheads are. Across the Top 14,

English Premiership and United Rugby Championship, tighthead props tend to be in the top five-ish positions by salary. They're often in the second/third-highest wage earners in the Top 14, which is a league that seriously values scrummaging and almost literally pays for their players by weight – it's like they're buying meat from a wholesaler. The increase in demand and wages for tighthead props has in some small part been a result of societal factors. Put simply, a lot of boys and girls are quite happy to look like scrummaging monsters on the pitch, but not so keen off it. The author of this book once spoke to a student who was completing a degree in sports science (another vague scientific reference that's perfectly in keeping with this book's approach to facts and referencing). As part of his thesis, he assessed the role of societal factors on rugby in the Welsh valleys. One of the reasons for the lack of tightheads, in certain parts of Wales, was partly down to how men now perceive their bodies and a resulting desire to be fashionable. Squeezing into a pair of trendy denim jeans is now more important than it is to squeeze into the gap between the hooker and loosehead. The role of the tighthead has changed hugely, and to the author of this book they're the most important players on the pitch, especially at Test level.

We love you tightheads, even though denim-focused fashion designers clearly don't.

Decision – Tightheads have always been awesome

HOOKER

Hookers, the search term that makes social media's porn bots absolutely lose their shit. The change in the role of a modern hooker has been massive. What was once a set-piece-based position has now become the role of an additional openside flanker – or even inside-centre. The ball-carrying responsibilities of a hooker have changed enormously, with many modern hookers often being left out in the 'wider pods' where there's greater opportunity to carry into space, and smaller players. Many modern hookers demolish more wings than a pisshead at Nando's – think Dan Sheehan for Ireland or Dane Coles for New Zealand.

You could argue that the first modern blueprint for a modern-day hooker was Keith Wood. Wood did it all, and to this day remains one of the all-time greats in that position. Wood was unique in that he scrummaged, threw and carried to a very high level, something that isn't always the case with modern hookers. With fewer scrums and fewer lineouts in the modern game, the offensive role of hookers has led to a generation who are happier carrying the ball, rather than throwing it into the lineout. While we're talking about lineout throwing, it still seems weird that the hooker is given the role for throwing at all. Other than the tighthead, they're the only players on the pitch who actually spend large periods of time wrestling/scrummaging with other players, using both arms and shoulders. But then they're expected to use those same arms to execute an accurate throw with a perfect spiral. It's like asking Luke Littler to hit a 180, but only after doing 20 reps with a 15kg dumbbell – while simultaneously getting his head kicked in.

Decision – Rugby is better in the f'ing modern day

LOOSEHEAD

In the old days, there was less of a difference between the tighthead and loosehead. The only difference really was that one faced two players in the scrum and the other one. Oh, and their names are different, of course. One prop sound like they have their head screwed in so tightly that it causes migraines, while the other has their head just lolling around on their shoulders like a newborn baby on the back of a roided-up rodeo bull. Often, they were just called props, with little differentiation. But that's just like calling all underpants, underpants, when there's a clear difference between the live-hard die-young 'boxer short' and the understated, bullet-proof practicality of the 'Y-front'.

Labelling both props as just props is something that still rather infuriatingly happens today. You'll regularly see modern-day team sheets labelled with 'prop'. Wikipedia is also a serial offender for leaving off the loose and tight. While they may be labelled the same, the loosehead is no longer solely a scrummaging position. They, of course, do have to scrummage, and scrummage well, but now many teams use their loosehead as a primary carrying option in their pod systems. Plus, they're also often used as primary 'jackalers' in defence. What was once seen as a rather plodding position, for players who had a higher fat content than a Wagyu steak, is now one of the most mobile roles in the pack. Players such as Gethin Jenkins, of Wales, revolutionised the position and made the rugby-watching public realise that your loosehead is at a rather loose end if they're merely focusing only on scrummaging.

Decision – Rugby is better in the f'ing modern day

LOCK

The role of an old-fashioned lock was simple: jump in the lineout, without assistance, then replicate the behaviour of a 1980s doorman (unlicensed) in between those lineouts. While having dexterous hands was always a key skill, those hands also had to be able to grab throats and punch faces on demand. That element of the lock's role hasn't been diluted that much, in reality, even at Test level. Think of Eben Eztebeth, for instance, a man who with two hands could constrict three good-sized anacondas. But there's far more to the modern lock than that. Their role, of course, still involves a level of grunt, and cleaning rucks remains a primary focus. But since the advent of players such as Brodie Retallick, locks are often the creative distributors in the first or second pod.

But if you really want to know much how the role of a lock has changed, you need merely see how much they're paid in the pro ranks. No matter which leagues you look at, locks are always in the top of the highest earners. Locks earn the big bucks because there simply aren't many people over 6ft 6in tall wandering the Earth. Even when they do find those giant freaks roaming the planet, they also have to be over 18 stone, enjoy getting hurt and, more importantly, be able to run for 80 minutes and stay injury-free while doing so. Massive Test-level locks are largely found in those countries with large populations and player pools. It's simply a matter of probability. The more people there are in your country, the more chance there is of you creating a load of throat-grabbing circus freaks. See South Africa as an example, where the entire country is just one giant showroom for monsters.

Decision – Rugby is better in the f'ing modern day

BLINDSIDE FLANKER

While the wider role of back-row forwards has changed since the game turned pro, and some teams try to play opensides at 6, the traditional role of the 6/blindside flanker has remained the same. Ideally, you need to be 6ft 2-ish, about 16 stone, and have a level of aggression that would have seen you through a solid stint in the Colombian prison system in the mid-1980s. The only real change to their role is that locks/second rows have been trying to take their jobs. 'Bloody locks coming over here and taking our jobs,' is a regular chant heard at the BTU – the Blindside Trade Union's summer congress.

The selection of lock/6 hybrids has become very fashionable in recent years. The increased lineout options from selecting a taller 6 has become very enticing for Test coaches and club-level coaches. The rise in the 'hybrid lock' has been especially popular at club level, where tightening budgets have meant that specialist players have been largely priced out of the system in certain positions. But while lock/6 hybrids are undoubtedly efficient and essentially the air fryer of rugby, you can't beat a proper 6. Literally, they'd absolutely fucking batter you, and all of your family, if you tried.

Decision – Rugby was better in the f'ing old days

NUMBER 8

The number 8. A once proud position dominated by tall, heavy ball carriers who could accelerate faster than post-Brexit inflation, but are now disappearing faster than polar bears – which isn't perhaps that surprising given their similarity in size and aggression levels. But with the reduction in scrums and the stability of scrums, the number 8 has become a role played by hybrid back-row players who are happy at 6, 7 or 8. With a legit number 8 probably having fewer than three heavy carries from scrums per game, the desire to pick lighter, more mobile players (who can contribute more in other aspects of the game) became too much for most coaches to ignore. It has meant that proper number 8s have gone the way of other once popular jobs – number 8s have essentially become rugby's 'milkmen'. As an aside, number 8s would make amazing milkmen – should that role ever become popular again. Massive hands for carrying five pints per hand, and if you don't pay the bill they run straight through the wall to your house, wind you, and then take the money that they're owed.

Decision – Rugby was better in the f'ing old days

OPENSIDE

Few roles in rugby have changed as much since the amateur days than that of the openside. What was once the link between the backs and forwards became a role more suited to cage fighters. Before the game turned pro, openside flankers were regarded as ball players, forwards who played like backs. But then came the 'jackal' and everything changed. The 'jackal', the chance to steal the ball on the floor by placing your body over it, changed everything. It meant that the nimblest player in the pack, who used to use that speed to fuse with the back line, now used that speed to get into the 'jackal' position before anyone else.

It has been a strange job transition for openside flankers. They're still one of the most revered players on the pitch, but now it's purely through a defensive lens, not attacking. The defensive tag for opensides is also further reinforced by the number of tackles that modern opensides make in a game. Even in the mid-2010s, many opensides would receive a player-of-the-match award for making 20 tackles in 80 minutes. Now, many back-row forwards are making 30-plus, which is absolutely insane – there are combine harvesters that don't chop up that much stuff in 80 minutes. Deciding whether the defensive role of the modern openside outweighs the more attacking role of the old-school openside is difficult. It's like choosing between Strongbow and Strongbow Dark Fruits, which the author of this book refuses to do.

Decision – It's a draw

SCRUM-HALF

The level of shit that scrum-halves talk will never

change (as referenced in this author's previous book). If you swept up the amount of shit that a typical scrum-half talks in a typical day, you could easily use it to not only grow roses commercially but dominate that market globally. However, while they have always talked an epic level of crap, their role has also involved taking on a load of crap that many of them probably didn't want in the first place. What was once a position judged by the quality of their pass, is now a role judged by the quality of their box-kick. With pods of forwards ever closer to the scrum-half, in attacking play, the role of the silky, long, perfect spiral pass is something that you'll now only see on VHS.

It's a shame really. Scrum-halves used to be famous for their pass and often had their own unique style. The dive pass was a key feature of rugby from the 1970s through to the 1990s, and while it did little to improve the ball flight and assistance to the outside-half, it looked fucking awesome. Now, with many scrum-halves feeding pods of forwards with short passes, often end on end, the precision of their pass is only fully appreciated when passing deep into their own goal line for 'exit plays' or from first-phase plays – namely the lineout.

What's quite interesting about the position of scrum-half is that the size of them seems to change like fashions in clothing. There can be decades where scrum-halves are the traditional 5ft 6in to 5ft 10in tall, only for the occasional 6ft 2in scrum-half to appear out of nowhere – Joost van der Westhuizen, Terry Holmes and Mike Phillips being notable examples. While scrum-halves are as skilled as they always have been, their role was more greatly appreciated in the old days, and it would be fantastic to return to the days of the passing 9.

Decision – Rugby was better in the f'ing old days

FLY-HALF

Outside-halves are the monarchs of rugby, in that they had it great for years, barely had to get their fingers dirty and now they're having to muck in like the fucking rest of us. Prior to 1996, if you saw a fly-half with any mud on them, it was probably a face-mask. If you combine all of the tackles made by outside-halves in the 1970s, 80s and 90s it's less than zero. But that wasn't their role and nor did it need to be. Prior to the advent of professional defensive systems in the early 2000s, outside-halves had more room to move than buffalo in pre-Columbus America – now they have less room to move than a battery chicken. The modern role of the 10 has become more about control than creation. You simply can't sidestep like Phil Bennett when Pieter-Steph du Toit is standing in your channel – you can try, but you'll end up looking like a pile of dirty washing on the floor.

One of the issues with the understanding of modern rugby is that many older fans still want outside-halves to play like they did in the 1970s, even though the space is no longer there. It's like yearning to walk out of your house and see nothing but open fields, only to see three high streets and 12 vape shops on each. The role of the 10 has changed undeniably, but while that creativity has maybe now been adopted in other roles (wider in the back line), it's quite sad to see outside-halves being reduced from the samurai swords they once were to the penknives of modern rugby.

Decision – Rugby was better in the f'ing old days

WING

In the old days, wing was the position once ruled by those who had to double check whether they were tall enough to go on a fairground ride or a waterslide. Of course, even if they weren't tall enough, they were often fast enough to duck under the safety barrier, evade the security and jump on the ride, regardless. But that all changed once Jonah Lomu appeared (as we mentioned previously). If it truly came down to a challenge to decide who altered the game more, Webb Ellis or Jonah Lomu, Lomu would simply pick up Ellis and use him as the ball. Lomu changed everything. But while wings have obviously got bigger as a rule, it isn't solely the domain of the massive beasts that media will often have you believe.

In the early 2020s, South Africa started to reintroduce the smaller wing as a matter of course, not the exception. Whereas players like Shane Williams and Jason Robinson were once regarded as one-offs from a bygone era, Rassie Erasmus made the undersized wing seem like an asset, not a risk. Players such as Cheslin Kolbe, etc. have made the rugby public realise that speed and footwork is still one of the wing's core roles – especially in an era where kicking away large percentages of possession to back-three players is often necessary. Rugby was always pitched as a game for all shapes and sizes. And while that may no longer be true in some positions, it still remains true on the wing.

Decision – Wings have always been cool as f**k

INSIDE-CENTRE

This is the position that's arguably the hardest to define and one that changes on an almost weekly basis – let alone between decades. Are inside-centres supposed to be a second outside-half or a second blindside flanker? Are they there to create or to destroy? Inside-centres come in more shapes and sizes than takeaway coffees – and good ones are just as pricey. The argument over whether a 12 is a creator or a destroyer is largely due to the fact that the 12 has such big defensive and attacking responsibilities. The 12 is usually one of the most robust defenders in the whole team, yet also receives stacks of touches of the ball in attack. At club level, even at pro level, you could argue that 'ball-playing' 12s are still a viable option, where there remains enough space for meaningful creativity. The same cannot be said at Test level, where openside flankers are the speed of centres, centres are the speed of wings, and wings are the speed of Japanese motorcycles. At Test level in the modern game, there's no space in the 10 and 12 channels and, as a result, the role of a 12 has become a 'gainline-first' position.

This isn't to say that you can only pick a 'big lump' at 12, but they must be able to perform that core role. It's in this regard that quality 12s are some of the rarest players in the game. There are plenty of 12s who can run through poured concrete. There are plenty of 12s who can kick. There are plenty of 12s that can pass. But there are very few who can do all three. And that is why the 'triple-threat' inside-centre is the snow tiger of rugby. At any one time in global rugby there are only ever three or four genuine world-class 12s playing at any time. They're not only rarer than hens' teeth, but they're also rarer than a hen's Invisalign.

Decision – Rugby is better in the f'ing modern day

OUTSIDE-CENTRE

For the rugby purist, the outside-centre has always been the glamour position in the back line. Yes, the outside-halves may always get to shake hands with the monarch of the time and get invited to nibble sushi at the palace, but 13s are the real royalty of rugby. At 13 you must be the most adaptable defender on the pitch, able to stop anything that comes your way, but also have the top-end gas to chase a good-quality pickpocket on London's Oxford Street. Being able to read the attack has always been the role of a 13, regardless of the era. But in the amateur days the threats were more linear and ran in more predictable patterns. In the amateur era the defensive role of a 13 focused far more on being able to 'drift' effectively – which is a tough skill in its own right.

Things are far more complicated for the modern-day 13. Reading a modern-day attack is like picking up a book where the pages have been put in in the wrong order. In the 13 channel there are both forwards and backs, running at angles across both your openside vision and blindside vision. Plus, you must master arguably the hardest part of the modern defensive gameplan – when to blitz out of the line and when not to. In the modern game, it's often the 13 who has to decide whether to charge out into the passing channel and make a 'spot tackle' or to stay in the defensive shape. If a 13 makes the correct defensive read, they become Bruce Willis; if they get it wrong, they become Bruce Forsyth. Modern 13s are the absolute shit and don't get the respect they deserve.

Decision – Rugby is better in the f'ing modern day

FULL-BACK

Polar bears often live in areas as big as 50,000 square miles and travel up to 19 miles a day. That is what it's like to play full-back. Yes, you often have acres of space from which to attack, but you also have to defend that entire space. Plus, full-backs are also unique in that there's often no defender behind them – they are the last defender. If you ever see a full-back performing a role in a pantomime, don't ever shout 'they're behind you', as they won't have a clue what you're talking about. They'll then probably run straight into whatever audience member is standing in front of them and tackle them around the legs – senior citizen at the matinee or not.

One area that hasn't changed for full-backs, regardless of era, is the need to be more fearless in the air than an Avro Lancaster pilot. Jumping in the air and not knowing how you'll land is not for everyone, and marks out full-backs as one of the bravest players on the pitch. Many rugby supporters often regard opensides as the most fearless players on the pitch – but full-backs aren't far behind. Perhaps the most interesting change in the skillset of full-backs comes in their attacking role. Virtually every decade, rugby tends to switch between favouring attacking full-backs over more defensive full-backs. These switches in the desired skillsets are usually the result of changes to the laws of kicking itself, or often breakdown interpretations. In the late 2000s the ball became so hard to retain at the breakdown that most teams would rather kick the ball away than risk losing it or conceding a penalty. It resulted in what was called 'kick-tennis', that being an unfair name because tennis as sport is great, whereas rugby's 'kick-tennis' was shitter than Donald Trump – in fact it was shitter than Donald Trump's actual shit.

If you were to pick two full-backs who summed up the amateur vs pro era, you could argue that JPR Williams and Christian Cullen represent the debate perfectly – even through Cullen's career came at the very beginning of the pro era. If the author of this book had to pick between the two, it would be Cullen. But I wouldn't want to break that news to the late, great, legendary Mr JPR Williams, for fear of him absolutely battering me – he could, of course, stitch you back together afterwards though.

Decision – It's a draw

THE BENCH

To many a bench is a very sedentary object. Somewhere to sit in a park or at the beach. Somewhere to admire the view or overfeed already portly pigeons. But the bench in modern rugby is a far less sedentary entity and something that has had a massive impact on rugby in recent years. When rugby began, benches were something that Webb Ellis merely plonked his ass on while changing – as there were no substitutions. In the old days, if a player was injured, they went off and no one else came back on. One can only imagine how injured you had to be back then to leave the pitch in an acceptable manner. Some players probably went off carrying their own faces. As we entered the late 1960s, replacements were then allowed for injuries. Weirdly, back then, the replacements often weren't allowed to be dressed in their kit on the sideline; they had to sit in the stands until a doctor had given them the all-clear to take the pitch.

What started as four replacements allowed in the 1970s-ish, became seven, and then in the late 2000s switched up to eight per team. In the 2020s, the role of 'subs' became hugely important and largely introduced the idea of all 23 players being of equal billing. The equal billing also led to a rebranding of the bench to 'finishers', which seems weird now, as we no longer refer to the bench using any words at all, but instead use digits, numbers, almost decimals.

The 2020s in rugby has seen the same labelling system adopted as that applied to mid-sized saloons by European vehicle manufacturers in the 1990s. Prior to the 1990s, cars used to be called things like the 'Cavalier', 'Sierra', 'Orion', only for them to be largely replaced by 3 Series, A4, etc. Rugby has now gone the same way with the racy 6:2, the spacious family 5:3, or the radical 7:1. While the bench in the modern era always had to contain three specialist front-row players (for safety reasons), to continue to the rather tortuous use of the car metaphor, rugby no longer has more seats in the front than in the back. It has now got six responsible, dependable parents up front and only enough room in the back for two utility children.

The use of GPS data has also had a massive impact on how the bench is used. There was a time when front-row forwards and scrum-halves played until they either vomited or stopped running entirely. But with GPS data, coaches are now able to accurately map when certain players and positions have dropped below their peak-performance level (usually around the 55-minute mark for front-row forwards, a little later in the game for scrum-halves).

Having access to so many replacements has its benefits for player welfare. On player welfare grounds, especially with regards to HIAs (Head Injury Assessments) there's absolutely no way that rugby can have fewer replacements – the number will increase if anything. The introduction of mass replacements in one go (i.e. the Bomb Squad in South African rugby) has also helped supporters understand the true importance of front-row forwards. There was a time when props and hookers entered the pitch with very little mention. Other than their immediate families, no one even noticed if they'd gone on to the pitch. The big fanfares used to be solely reserved for new backs coming on to the pitch, whereas now, props enter the pitch like it's in the WWE (World Wrestling Entertainment) or the glory days of the Roman Colosseum – which is genuinely fantastic and deserved.

But the changes to the role of replacements haven't all been positive. More substitutions mean that there are fitter, faster players on the pitch at all times – which on the face of it sounds great, but it isn't. Rugby needs space on the pitch to create line breaks, as without space there are fewer opportunities to attack and fewer opportunities to break down the defence. In short, rugby needs more tired players and missed tackles, not fewer. With regards to player safety, extra replacements has helped the game, but in terms of the way the game is played – not so much.

Decision – It's a difficult problem to solve

PLAYER AWARDS

It doesn't matter in what era you played or watched, backs and back-row forwards always win player of the year. It may be that they have nicer haircuts, ears that don't look like some weird dried vegetables, or simply because they score more tries and have more attacking touches per match, but for some reason backs and back-row forwards always get the end-of-year trophies. This doesn't just apply at Test level; it also happens at club level. When was the last time you saw an 18-stone prop, bulging out of their pristine white shirt, sporting a club tie that has more chance of wrapping around the belly of a basking shark, win player of the season? It simply does not happen. If you look through any World Player of the Year list, the players who do the heavy lifting during the season get to lift absolutely fuck all when it comes to the end of the season.

Front-row forwards and locks are like the bees of the rugby world. Yes, they're scary. Yes, you're often best running away from them. With some of them, any interaction could cause breathing problems and put you in hospital for 24 hours. But, without the front-row forwards and locks, rugby's natural order ceases to exist. If you see a prop or a lock, give them a hug. Or buy them some carbs. Or better still, vote for them to win some kind of award. They fully deserve it.

Decision – It's a draw (front-row forwards and locks have always been treated like second-class citizens)

SUPPORTERS

A QUICK WORD ON SUPPORTERS

Rugby supporters are rugby. Without them it's just 30 people playing a game that fits in somewhere between frisbee and fighting. Supporters keep both local rugby and professional rugby in business. Though the introduction of TV and social media has somewhat altered the role of supporters, they remain its heartbeat. Whether you watch in the stands, on TV, once a year or every week, this book doffs its hat to you, you beautiful people.

STADIUM SUPPORTERS

The stadium supporter is the traditional supporter. The OG. Those who buy a ticket, season ticket, a programme, a pint and a pie. They are the lifeblood of rugby at both Test and club level. But especially at club level. At Test level you'll get plenty of supporters who will attend single Test matches and pay a lot of money for the privilege, but that isn't the case at club level. Stadium supporters tend to favour matches that kick off at set times, predictable times – the 2pm kick-off being a prime example. They tend to be supporters that no longer play the game and have no further commitments within the game – hence are able to attend regular kick-off times. This may seem like a trivial detail, but it makes all the difference when it comes to scheduling matches. Without stadium supporters it doesn't matter how many TV supporters you have, the optics look bad, as the stands look like a supermarket shelf during the first few weeks of Covid.

Decision – Rugby supporters have always been f'ing awesome

TV SUPPORTERS

It seems weird to differentiate between supporters who watch rugby in the stadium and those who watch on TV/social media, but they're increasingly different groups of people. And without wishing to come across as overly capitalist – they all have a different economic value to the game. The TV supporter is the new supporter, the nouveau riche and disrespected in the same manner. The TV supporter is often labelled as the 'armchair supporter' in a rather derogatory tone – but often they contribute more money to rugby than the stadium supporter. TV supporters are the reason why many rugby matches occur at unusual times that fit in with TV schedules and multimatch formats. These are the supporters who often get blamed for fixtures kicking off at weird times, but are often contributing more to the overall financial pot of rugby than the traditional supporter. For example, if a TV supporter has £50-ish a month of rugby subscriptions per season, that's £600-ish of income for televised rugby, which is more than plenty of season tickets in the world of club rugby.

Decision – Rugby supporters have always been f'ing awesome

THE PLAYER-SUPPORTER

The player-supporter is a rare beast, but a beautiful beast nonetheless. The rugby player-supporter still plays rugby and also watches it. They present a dichotomy, because they often play rugby at an amateur level at the same time as professional rugby is also kicking off. The rugby player-supporter is something that doesn't really occur in soccer and further differentiates the sports from each other. Very few soccer fans actually still play competitive soccer – but that's not the case in rugby. Plenty of rugby supporters actually still play the game and their games kick off at the same times as pro games. This may seem like a silly detail, but it's important. Irregular kick-offs, late matches on Saturdays, matches on Friday nights and Sunday afternoons suit this audience – and they can't be ignored. They are the true pure-bloods of rugby.

Decision – Rugby supporters have always been f'ing awesome

RISE OF THE RUGBY SNOB

A relatively new addition to rugby union is the rise of the rugby snob. We need to firstly clarify what a rugby snob is, as it may not be initially obvious. A rugby snob isn't a rich rugby supporter who looks down on a poor rugby supporter. It actually has nothing to do with money at all. The last decade or so has seen a new gang of rugby supporters develop, who only like the 'right' people watching the game. In essence, they don't like those who only turn up for the Test matches and then don't watch club rugby. If you do only go and watch Test rugby, then you're treated with the scorn afforded to 18th-century French nobility – and you'll be publicly executed on social media.

But this snobbery doesn't just apply to how many matches you go to watch, but also what you wear. To be a true rugby 'purist', you have to wear just a match shirt and/or possibly a scarf. If you wear a daffodil hat or have your face painted with anything jovial, then you are essentially treated like Imelda Marcos. Then there's music at rugby, which purists also really hate. Even though music permeates through every other aspect of our modern lives, for some reason it isn't allowed at rugby, where all fans must take a vow of silence – like modern rugby monks living on Caldey, Ireland. And whatever you do, don't get up and go to the toilet during the match, or buy a pint of lager. If you have to make a trip to the bog, and one single rugby purist is forced to get up out of their seat, then you'll immediately be added to the list of rugby's witches who should be burned at the stake. Rugby doesn't need rugby snobs, and it never has.

Decision – Rugby was better in the f'ing old days

OFFICIAL SUPPORTERS' CLUBS

Official supporters' clubs have been a tremendous addition to rugby. Yes, rugby has arguably always had cohorts of fans who have represented supporters in one way or another, but the modern supporters' club is way more than that. The modern supporters' club is the ethical compass of most rugby clubs. They're not interested in money, and they're not interested in any other club. Their sole purpose is protecting their club from negative external and internal influences. Most supporters' clubs meet with their club boards on a regular basis and are part of the club's machinery. They also do a great job of promoting their teams on social media and in some instances do a better job than the clubs themselves. There's something both refreshing and reassuring about having supporters' clubs with such prominent roles in rugby at all levels – and long may it continue.

Decision – Rugby is better in the f'ing modern day

FEMALE SUPPORTERS

It's way off the mark to suggest that, once upon a time, rugby didn't have female supporters. It has always had hardcore female supporters. The author of this book's mother being one. She knows more about rugby than plenty. But in the old days, women didn't go to the rugby, they were taken there by their husbands. It seems archaic when looking back, but most rugby clubs didn't even have women in the club before, during or after a match. Their only representation was either behind the bar or in the kitchen – making food for the male players. Golf clubs used to get the grief for having a men-only policy, but rugby wasn't far behind.

Thankfully that's no longer the case. Far from it, in fact. The author of this book spends quite a lot of time on social media chatting to women. And before my wife reads this and swings something blunt at the back of my head – that's with reference to chatting with women about rugby. The number of replies to rugby posts that come from women is probably just under a 40:60 split between men and women (40 per cent women vs 60 per cent men), something that simply wouldn't have been the case even 30 years ago. Female supporters genuinely feel like the equal of men in rugby support, and it's great to see.

Decision – Rugby is better in the f'ing modern day

KIDS

Kids as supporters have always existed. Whether you're watching rugby from the 50s, 60s, 70s or 80s, kids have always been visible in rugby – often sitting on the shoulders of their dad, who's had four pints and is swaying like a shitty lineout lift. But children's role as supporters has changed radically in the pro age. They are arguably the most important supporters in the ground and much of rugby is now dedicated to them. Years ago, kids went to rugby to watch rugby, where the whole day out was targeted at their dads (i.e. rugby and beer). That is no longer the case. Much of rugby TV content, club activity and supporters' club activity is aimed at children specifically. It's great to see kids in rugby given the same attention and consideration as the adults who take them. And it's about time too, as most of them are the same size as scrum-halves and therefore deserve the same level of respect. Most children are, of course, far more well-behaved than scrum-halves and talk way less nonsense. So, the point becomes even more well-balanced.

Decision – Rugby is better in the f'ing modern day

CORPORATE SUPPORTERS

There are back-row forwards from the 1970s who didn't take as much of a kicking as corporate rugby supporters do. The corporate supporter is, of course, a relatively new addition to rugby. Since the day that rugby turned pro, it has needed money, and corporate tickets bring in that money. Corporate boxes bring in absolute fortunes for many teams, and unions, and their reputation as not being proper rugby supporters is very unfair. Yes, you could argue that the corporate sponsor at the top, the one buying the box, has little interest. Do big multinationals have a genuine interest in rugby? Probably not. But, largely, the people who are invited to those boxes are very interested in the game.

The author of this book's experiences of corporate boxes is that they're mostly proper fans who were lucky enough to get an invite. What's more, most of the people in rugby boxes seem very grateful for the day out and treat it as a one-off experience. It's not as if these people then don't watch another single game of rugby until they receive the next £500 invite to an all-you-can-eat in the Principality Stadium. But perhaps most important is that rugby really needs that money and corporate sponsors pay way over the odds for the service that's being delivered. So, the next time you see a 'corporate supporter' having a good day out, don't scowl, smile – they're helping keep rugby in the black, while consuming three bottles of red.

Decision – Rugby is better in the f'ing modern day

AWAY TRIPS

Away trips are a key part of rugby and always will be. But the true era of the away trip was definitely in the amateur era. It may be that rugby supporters now have so many more opportunities to watch rugby in the modern day, that away trips have lost their edge slightly. It may also be that social media has meant that what goes on tour, never stays on tour any more. But the tales of away trips in the modern era seem to be far tamer. As an example, a rugby tour left from the author of this book's local rugby club in the 1970s. They went to Paris during the Six Nations. After the trip, one of the gents said he'd never go back to Paris, because the last time he was there 'he caught fire'. While another, on the same trip, didn't think he'd be allowed back in Paris due to him having 'accidentally spat on a tiger'. There was also a story of a teacher from a local school who skipped a working school day to attend a match in

Scotland. Every preparation was made so that no one from the school knew where he was going, on that last Friday in term time, only for him to get snapped by a photographer and feature on the front cover of *Rugby World* magazine – we know the latter story is 100 per cent true, because it was the father of this very author.

Decision – It's a draw – away trips have always been cool

MEDIA

TRADITIONAL VS NEW MEDIA

The demise of rugby in traditional media is arguably one of the biggest changes that has ever happened to the game – newspapers being the most notable loser. It isn't exclusive to rugby, of course, as it has affected every aspect of information. But we are talking about rugby in this book, so here we go. Newspapers were for over 100 years the principal manner in which supporters engaged with rugby news (later followed by radio and TV). Even with the introduction of radio and TV, most rugby news was conveyed by papers. But then that all changed with social media. Suddenly, clubs and national teams started putting information directly on to social media via their own accounts and didn't really need so much interaction with the papers and journalists. It also meant that the information was no longer the sole property of a limited number of writers. Now, we all have access to the info, not just those who were lucky enough to be invited to a press conference.

It changed the game. It meant that having access to information was no longer the 'game'; now it's about what you do with it. The advent of social media created a new generation of rugby content, not just from traditional rugby writers, but also from online content creators. Accounts such as Squidge (behind which are the brilliant Owen brothers) created a new form of rugby media. The rise of the online content creator meant that people could create stuff in real-time, without having to wait for it to be published on a Sunday, for instance. It also meant that rugby content could become far more micro. Now, every club can have their own channel, and so too can every fan. This isn't to say that non-traditional rugby content has totally replaced traditional content in the modern age – it hasn't and never will. And there are plenty of writers who dabble in both paper and digital. But as a whole, rugby media feels far more balanced in the modern day. With more access to more information, for more people – which can never be a bad thing.

Decision – Rugby is better in the f'ing modern day

PLAYER ABUSE VIA SOCIAL MEDIA

Social media has had a hugely positive influence on rugby. It has allowed access to information to all, and for all to be allowed to create with that information. But it hasn't all been positive. Some of the abuse that players receive is a genuinely serious subject. Players have always received criticism. All people in all sports do. All people in all jobs do. But prior to social media, players only really took criticism from a select number of journalists, TV stations, former players or maybe the odd shout from a pisshead in a local pub. There were unwritten rules to the criticism, and checks and balances that kept the criticism to a reasonable level-ish. This isn't to say that traditional media didn't cross the line; they did, and there are tons of examples of it. But there's a difference between saying 'I hope your career dies a death' and 'I hope your kids do the same'. Social media has given direct access to players in a way that most of us simply didn't have unless we knew where they lived or had their actual phone number. As a result, social media has allowed some supporters to infiltrate players' social spaces and the inner workings of their lives – which obviously isn't a good thing.

Decision – Rugby was better in the f'ing old days

THE RISE OF THE PODCAST VS RADIO

Prior to the podcast, rugby was a very visual medium. It did, of course, have representation on radio. Indeed, the author of this book was part of a rugby radio show for a few years with the brilliant Rick O'Shea, and Rhodri Jones, at BBC Radio Wales. But largely, if you wanted to engage with rugby, you had to watch it. The rugby podcast changed that overnight. Suddenly, you could listen to rugby content 24/7 from all over the world. The variety of rugby podcasts now available to supporters is staggering. There are more rugby podcasts on planet Earth than there are species of insects – this is not true.

The podcasts are largely split into three: those podcasts created by official news outlets and leagues, those from former players and those from supporters. Podcasts from official news outlets and leagues tend to be more 'official' (as you'd expect). The former player podcasts tend to offer a more humorous approach and often give greater insight into rugby from a professional player's perspective. Then there are the supporters' podcasts, which for the author of this book are the most interesting. No official media source will ever know as much about a single professional rugby team or club than the diehard supporter. An official media podcast may be able to give you the birthday of a player, but the supporters will be able to tell you where those player's birthmarks are actually located on their body. Some of the detail delivered by supporters' podcasts are mind-blowing and so invaluable if you work in the rugby content industry. Long live the rugby pod.

Decision – Rugby is better in the f'ing modern day

PUNDITRY

As rugby players became more professional and more detailed in their role as players, it's no surprise that the modern rugby pundit has done the same. They are, after all, largely the same people. Modern punditry is almost unrecognisable from how it was in the amateur era. One aspect of the pundit's career that's rarely talked about is how competitive a sector it is. It's arguably more competitive than playing on the pitch itself. There are thousands of professional rugby players in the world, and yet only tens of jobs available in the media. If you want to keep your job, you have to be good. Plus, every season there's a new batch of retirees, with newer stories, newer insights and fewer wrinkles, just waiting to take that pay cheque from the incumbent. It's a far more difficult gig than many supporters give pundits credit for.

Decision – Rugby is better in the f'ing modern day

ON-PITCH INTERVIEWS

On-pitch interviews are tricky things to watch and to be a part of. We all want to hear what players think, but not when they're breathing like a bulldog that's lost its asthma pump. For some reason, TV companies think that the public want to know what the players think during the 25 seconds that they leave the pitch – which creates a sub-optimum situation for all concerned. It's very difficult to think when you're struggling to breathe, and, as a result, the answers from players are very brief, neutral and sometimes unintelligible. Rugby and most other sports are one of the few examples in life where we ask people questions in situations where they're struggling for oxygen. It's very rare to see anyone being interviewed when they've literally just had a punctured lung repaired or just been rescued from a sunken crab boat. The players don't like doing the interviews, supporters don't like watching them and the interviewers don't appear to enjoy it either.

Save it for after the match, when breathing levels have returned to normal.

Decision – Rugby was better in the f'ing old days

RUGBY COMMENTARY

Rugby commentary has always been of a high standard. There's never been a period in rugby history when you look back at TV coverage or listen to radio coverage and think, *What the fuck are they talking about?* Something that will undoubtedly be said, and rightly so, when people read this book. Some will say that Bill McClaren is the undoubted king, and they may be right. Eddie Butler was also mesmeric behind the mic, and no one could voice-over a rugby montage like Mr Butler. But there are stacks of modern commentators who can more than hold their own against some of the legends behind the microphone.

Rugby commentators tend to fall within two camps: those who focus on the details of the match and those who focus on the use of creative/descriptive language. The perfect spot is, of course, somewhere in the middle. Being a rugby commentator is tricky in many ways and something that they have in common with many of the world's most famous painters – in that many don't get the praise they deserve until they've passed away. While most commentators are alive, some supporters will always have a gripe over something that they may have said about their favourite player or with a perceived bias against their team. But when those commentators die, it's as if all the negativity is boiled away and you're just left with the good stuff. My apologies if any rugby commentators read this. I wish you a long, verbose and happy life. Cheers, Paul.

Decision – Rugby commentators have always been f'ing awesome

REPLAYS

Replays are now as much a part of rugby as the ball itself. Nothing happens without the say-so of replays. But it hasn't always been that way. Up until the professional era, replays were a joyous part of rugby, used to celebrate beauty, innovation and skill – whereas now they seem to have become a shitty stick with which to beat rugby's imperfections. In the amateur era, replays largely showed exquisite handling, whereas now they show handling in the ruck, or a slipped bind in the scrum. All of this has led to the game being refereed far more accurately, but arguably less attractively. It depends on what we/you want from rugby. Do you want to be perfect and pedantic? Or loose and laden with lies?

The reality is that rugby has always been imperfect and, in the old days (without the heavy use of replays), we either accepted it or ignored it. If you saw replays of your top ten favourite tries from the 1970s and 1980s, very few would now stand as a try. If the overt use of replays existed during that famous Barbarians match, then the famous try wouldn't have. Replays in rugby are like Elon Musk in that they initially seemed okay and could benefit us, but increasingly seem like they're ruining stuff.

Decision – Rugby needs f'ing replays, but maybe not so many

TV

TV is more important to rugby than many in rugby would like to admit. Many loathe that TV dictates kick-off times and has reduced the number of people buying tickets at certain levels of rugby. But rugby has changed a lot in the professional era and TV has been key to that. Rugby clubs and Test nations could once survive on ticket sales, and 'pies and pints', when they didn't have to pay individual players £250k a year. That is no longer the case. TV money for many teams, and nations, is the bulk of the revenue stream. For some leagues and teams, TV revenue is as high as 70 per cent-ish.

Being dominated by TV revenue is not unique to rugby, of course, but nor is it without problems. Full TV coverage has for many fans ruined the atmosphere (especially with regards to away fans) and you could argue has reduced overall attendance figures in some leagues. TV has also led to the fragmentation of the commercial market to the point where many supporters need three packages to follow one sport. The reliance on money from TV has also had a massive impact on when matches are played. Kick-offs are no longer dictated by when it's most suitable for fans in a local market, but when it's suitable for wider markets – which often are very different. But, to put it simply, without TV there would be no professional rugby. It's as simple as that.

Decision – Rugby is better in the f'ing modern day

TV GRAPHICS

TV graphics have come a long way in rugby. In the amateur era, rugby graphics looked like they had been designed by very small children and were also being held in position on screen by those same small kids – which probably explained why the graphics often twitched on screen as their little arms got tired. In the modern area, they've come a long way. Now, every game is littered with 3D graphical representations of stats and info – which is key to developing the understanding of the sport for new and existing supporters. Yet for the author of this book, there remains a 'rugby graphic' bugbear. After decades of televised rugby and increases in technology, why do we still not have graphics on screen showing the weather? In a sport where the quality of play is largely determined by the quality of the weather, why don't we have a rain graphic, a wind graphic, a temperature graphic? All of this would help explain why passes are being dropped, why kicking percentages are lower than expected, etc. TV graphics still have some way to go, but they're a fantastic addition to the product.

Decision – Rugby is better in the f'ing modern day

STATS

You either love stats in rugby or you don't. Rugby stats didn't really exist in the amateur era. The only stats you had access to as a writer or supporter were the score, number of tries scored, goal kicks/conversions/drop-goals scored and the number of caps that each player had. That was literally it. Everything else discussed in rugby was just opinion. Prior to the use of stats, rugby opinions were usually based on which team 'wanted it more', which team 'turned up on the day' and a 'game of two halves', etc. The introduction of stats into rugby not only added depth to coaching and the public's understanding of rugby, but also meant that having a vague opinion on rugby was no longer enough. In the modern game, the quality of debate has improved enormously. Stats are the friend of the modern-day supporter and pundit. They encourage accuracy and dissuade lazy debates/opinions.

Decision – Rugby is better in the f'ing modern day

RUGBY IS A TWO-DEVICE SPORT

The way that supporters have viewed sport has changed hugely over the past 140 years. First, we used our eyes in a stadium, or at a local ground. Then we used our eyes via TV. Then we used our eyes via social media platforms. But all of those approaches have tended to focus on one use of media, rather than multiple. The problem is that rugby is no longer a game that can be fully appreciated using one type of media. The reality is that modern rugby is a game that requires both a wide angle and a narrow angle – which can only be achieved with two types of media platform or a split screen on the TV. You need the wide view to appreciate the backs and the space and a tight angle to see what's happening in the mauls, scrums, rucks, etc. This should be the next big jump for rugby media – a sports app for phones that just focuses on the maul, scrums, rucks, etc. This should be mandatory in stadiums, where many supporters leave some matches not really understanding why half of the decisions were given in the first place. Rugby is now a two-device game, and this progression needs to happen sharpish.

Decision – Rugby will be better in the future if they adopt this f'ing suggestion

GEOGRAPHY

RUGBY'S GEOGRAPHY

Don't panic, this isn't going to read like a GCSE textbook, even though the author of this book does own a few blazers with elbow patches. This bit of the book is a quick look at how small the game once was, how big it has become and how big it can realistically be in the future.

TEST RUGBY'S GEOGRAPHY

Rugby started locally, obviously. What was once a game played between private schools soon branched out into clubs – as many of the boys who played in schools back then wanted to continue when they left school. But as with most things that humans are involved with, word spreads and things can get competitive pretty quickly. All it takes is one person in England to say, 'We're great at this rugby stuff,' and another in Scotland to say, 'That's bollocks, we're better,' and, before you know it, about 150 years later you've got a Rugby World Cup.

Rugby's global spread largely came because of the British Empire. You could argue that it's one of the few silver linings of what otherwise is a very big, grey, shitty empirical cloud. With the Empire, rugby grew, and the impact of that can still be seen today with the likes of New Zealand dominating since they first set eyes on an oval ball. If you're not a Kiwi, the British taking a rugby ball to New Zealand can be viewed as a major mistake – as they've barely lost a damn match since.

Decision – Rugby is better in the f'ing modern day

CLUB RUGBY'S GEOGRAPHY

While Test rugby has obviously always had a wider reach, club/regional/provincial rugby hasn't. You could argue that until rugby went professional most supporters weren't really aware of the club rugby that was taking place beyond their borders. Supporters would, of course, be aware of the odd club from other nations, if they'd played Test teams on various tours – such as the British and Irish Lions, etc. But arguably before the advent of the Champions' Cup, or the original Super Rugby format, club rugby was quite an isolated affair. The author of this book, for instance (who admittedly isn't the sharpest), didn't realise that a Garry Owen up-and-under was named after the Garryowen rugby club in Limerick until he was about 18 years old.

This rather parochial approach to rugby is no longer the case, of course. Now you'll see fans who support their core team, and then also support teams in other leagues. You may find a hardcore Leicester Tigers fan who also supports the Lions in Johannesburg – if they have a particular love of super cats for instance.

Decision – Rugby is better in the f'ing modern day

PLAYER DISPERSAL

The interconnection and cross-fertilisation of the game across both Test and club rugby hasn't just affected rugby at an organisational level, it has had a major impact on the players also. The introduction of big TV deals and multi-country competitions has meant that players are now free to play wherever they like. In the 1940s and 1950s, it was rare for teams to have players from outside of the locality. Most players were home-grown – literally within walking distance for many. In the 1960s and 1970s, players began to stretch their legs a bit and began moving to clubs further afield. In Wales, for example, many chose the bright lights and moved to London Welsh – which was a club set up in London in 1885 for the Welsh expat community in London. On the 1971 British and Irish Lions tour, London Welsh had seven players selected.

But since the game has gone truly global, players can now play where they like and the local player is a rarity in many leagues. Many used to prefer club rugby, when it had the same ethos as Test rugby, as in you play for the club where you live. But that's the difference between the pro and amateur era. You now play where the money and the success is, which is the whole point of professional sport.

Decision – Rugby is better in the f'ing modern day

RESIDENCY AND PROJECT PLAYERS

Residency used to apply to housing, and DJs who got paid way too much money to play in clubs in Ibiza in the1990s. But in rugby union, it means something else. Residency in rugby used to mean that you could qualify to play for a country if you'd played rugby in that country for a set period. The qualification actually changed in 2022. From 2022, a player had to have played/lived in a country for 60 consecutive months. Prior to that, it was just 36 months. The 36-month time period felt too short and led to 'project players'. 'Project players' were those individuals who hadn't played for another nation, so could be moved to a club in another nation, and then after a three-year period of residency could play for that country. It essentially meant that Northern Hemisphere Test teams went 'project player' shopping in the Southern Hemisphere.

Interestingly, the same was not the case for Southern Hemisphere teams, who saw very little reason to go shopping in the Northern Hemisphere. The whole situation is tricky. How long does it take for someone to live in a particular country before they truly identify with that country? Do you even have to truly identify with something to even play for it? In some ways the rules over Test eligibility were set in the amateur era and have never been truly adapted for the global game where players can choose to play in any country they like. It's a very difficult problem with no easy solution. If you made the residency laws ten years, for example, a player would never be able to play for another country, as many players aren't lucky enough to have a ten-year career, even though they may well have fully adopted that country as their true home in a decade of living there. Conversely, if it were one year, a wealthy nation could buy all of the best players in the world, fill their club system with those players and then populate their Test teams with those players in a period of just 12 months. It would mean that money would then be able to buy Test rugby to an unacceptable degree.

Decision – Rugby was better in the f'ing old days

THE HYBRID CAREER AT CLUB LEVEL

There was a time in rugby where you played for one club (pretty much) and one country. It was linear and simple. You played for your local team, pretended there wasn't any money being placed in your boots at the end of the game, and got on with it. But that's no longer the case. Players now have multiple clubs over a career, playing in multiple countries and multiple leagues. Such is the desire and financial reward of playing in multiple countries that we've now seen the introduction of the career sabbatical.

Career sabbaticals used to be for accountants who wanted to take six months off, smoke ayahuasca then run through the Amazon, naked. But rugby players aren't allowed to do any of that, so most of them go to Japan for a season, sample sashimi and earn a fortune. The Japanese league isn't the same standard as many other professional leagues and is far less attritional. The author of this book was once told by a former All Black second row that in Japan he could clear entire rucks with just his hands. But while the 'career sabbatical' in Japan is largely viewed with some scepticism from rugby supporters, it's not without its benefits. It can seriously extend a player's career and add plenty of extra Test caps to a player's total – plus they get to earn some serious money in what can be a seriously short career.

Decision – Rugby is better in the f'ing modern day

THE HYBRID CAREER AT TEST LEVEL

In recent years, due to a change in the eligibility qualifications at World Rugby, we've also seen players being able to play for multiple countries. Until 1990-ish, players could do this anyway – which for some reason rarely gets talked about. If you were born in a country, had a parent from that country, or a had a grandparent from that country, you could play for that country –

you could switch allegiances without a stand-down period. Players such as Diego Domínguez did exactly that. He played for Argentina in 1989, then switched to Italy in 1991. In the late 1990s, the process changed to stop players switching willy-nilly at Test level – once you were capped by a nation, you were stuck. However, since January 2022, the eligibility rules have changed so players who have already been capped have the ability to switch nations if they meet these two criteria:

- Have served a stand-down period from international rugby for 36 months.
- Were born in the country to which they wish to transfer or have a parent or grandparent born in that country.

The change was made so that countries with smaller player resources could 're-cap' players who had essentially been snapped up by a bigger nation initially and then not selected them for three years or more. For example, if a player with a Samoan link had been capped by Australia initially but not played for three years, then they could play for Samoa. While the intentions were honourable and designed to make rugby a fairer place for smaller nations, it has, of course, been exploited by some of the larger nations – for whom the ruling wasn't intended. Many tier-one nations are now turning Test rugby into rugby 'eBay' – where you can bid on players with previous owners.

Decision – Rugby was better in the f'ing old days

SCHOOL-AGE RECRUITMENT

Rugby is a game of tactics. But, at both club and Test level, rugby's tactics have started to be planned and executed way before the whistle has blown. In some cases, five years before; in some instances, even longer. There was a time in rugby union where supporters would worry about losing players to another club or Test team when those players were in their early 20s – now it often happens in the early or mid-teens. In ten years' time, some teams and unions may be signing players directly from the womb, with a contract being pressed into their face as soon as they exit. Offers of private education, etc. are very difficult to ignore, especially when they're wrapped up with a career pathway into successful clubs/regions/provinces – and then, of course, the Test team that sits above it all. At under-20s level, it's a very savage business, where players must make the decision to play for their country of 'birth', or the country where they've received their free education and all of the benefits that come with it. It means that many players are making decisions on their Test career before they've even begun their club career.

Decision – Rugby was better in the f'ing old days

GRANDMOTHERS AND GRANDFATHERS

Grandmothers and grandfathers rarely have a role in most professional sports. At that sort of age, the focus tends to be on what's for tea, and what day the recycling/bins are going out. Yet in rugby, grandmothers and grandfathers play a significant role at Test level. In short, if your grandparents are from a certain country, you can play for that country. It used to be a perfectly acceptable qualification for rugby players. Up until the mid-1990s, if you as a player had a grandparent from a particular nation, you were 100 per cent welcomed as being from that country's lineage.

But then things went a bit weird. Namely in Wales, where they started to make up grandparents. That doesn't mean they were physically making up grandparents, on some kind of really sick production line (although the way things currently are in Welsh rugby, in 2025, many would happily accept such a scenario). They were making up the link to grandparents, via documentation. It became known as 'granny gate', and almost overnight having a grandparent link to a country was suddenly under question, when it really shouldn't be. If your grandparents are from a certain country, that's more than enough to play for that country, and the unnecessary scrutiny around the subject is irritating.

Decision – Rugby was better in the f'ing old days

RUGBY'S DESIRE TO GROW

In the amateur era, rugby knew what it was. It was a local game at club level, and a reasonably niche game at Test level – largely due to the fact that it was nearly quicker to travel to space than sail to Australia with 30 lads on a boat. But as with all pro sport, or any commercial enterprise for that matter, the desire to grow is infectious. When rugby turned pro in 1996 there were small groups of largely wealthy white men in their 50s who made their millions and then could buy and run a professional rugby team from well within the bounds of their wealth. Back then you could buy an English Premiership team for about six quid and then sign six shit-hot Kiwi backs and six shit-hot South African forwards for the same price as a meal deal at Spud U Like.

It's the 2010s where things got a little bit out of control. The ability for players to move to other leagues, often more wealthy leagues, drove up wage inflation in all of rugby. Club teams paying big money in France meant that teams in England had to follow suit and, with it, the phrase 'salary cap' had as much meaning to a CEO in rugby as 'celery-cap' would to a milliner. Throw in a global pandemic and rugby has become a game with aspirations that it simply cannot afford.

Rugby has always looked at soccer with envy and a desire to become like it. But rugby is nothing like soccer. They may have started from the same genesis, but they're nothing alike. Humans share 98.8 per cent of our DNA with the chimpanzee, but ask a chimpanzee to write a rugby column and it's absolutely fucking crap at it – they send it in late, covered in bananas, and often having wiped their ass with the laptop. Amateur rugby was not without its problems, but it was far easier to manage the budgets. Rugby needs to live within its means.

Decision – Rugby needs to get a f'ing grip of its finances

THE LONG TOUR

The long tour in rugby no longer exists, of course. Most Test tours are three Tests maximum; many are two Tests – which lead to very annoying 'drawn' outcomes. Even the Lions tours, which do of course include a stack of superb club games, aren't nearly as long as they were. In the early days, players would leave for rugby tours, and when they returned their four-year-old kids were now married and had four-year-old kids of their own. Some rugby tours left during the start of the Jurassic Period and returned for the wedding of Charles and Diana. The first British and Irish Lions tour in 1888 had 35 matches. They left in March and came back in November. If you did that now, you'd start the tour in the middle of *Britain's Got Talent*, miss the cricket season and then return for the first episode of *I'm a Celebrity Get Me Out of Here*. All of this was also done, of course, in the amateur period, so the players weren't even paid for playing the matches. The commitment involved from those players and their families was absolutely incredible – but unsustainable.

Decision – Rugby is better in the f'ing modern day

GLOBAL LEAGUES

As much as all rugby fans like to think of rugby as being the most important sport in the world, it really isn't. Hardly any of the world watches it and even less play it. It didn't really matter in the old days, when no one was getting paid. If there were 15 of you and 15 of us, we could play. But when 30 of those players needed to be paid, rugby had to widen its net to generate some cash. First, it started with local leagues, national unions, etc. But in the end that wasn't enough either. As the need for money grew, so did the need for rugby's boundaries to expand. In the 1990s/2000s, we saw the first true cross-border competitions begin – such as Super Rugby in the Southern Hemisphere, the European Cup in its various formats, and the Celtic League, as it was called then.

These multi-country leagues have been great for the game, especially for those countries with smaller populations. The income from the leagues has increased the number of eyes on TV screens and therefore the revenue generated. But beyond the financials, these hybrid leagues have created some of the finest rugby that we've ever seen. They allowed the best in the world to compete at club level, not just Test level, something that very few supporters had seen other than on 'Test tours'. The hybrid country leagues allowed a mix of all players from around the world to play each other on a weekly basis, but above all they allowed supporters from different countries to look beyond their boundaries, and skin colours, and discover new heroes from new countries. One minute your favourite player is from a small village in South Wales, the next he's from a small village in New South Wales.

These multi-border leagues do, of course, come with certain problems. The environmental cost is a worry, with flights being required for most fixtures. Plus, the kick-off times can be really weird. Especially in the version of Super Rugby that included South Africa, where sometimes you'd be watching a match being whistled before any birds had.

Decision – Rugby is better in the f'ing modern day

THE RISE OF THE PACIFIC ISLAND PLAYERS

Pacific Island players have always been influential in rugby – that is undeniable. One of the only redeeming features of Britain's Empire is that it took rugby to the Pacific Islands. In doing so they unleashed some of the most influential rugby nations in the world – arguably the most influential. For entire countries, some of which have the same populations as medium-sized towns in the UK, the Pacific Islands have essentially led rugby in a way that no other nations have. Per population, their impact is ridiculous and unrivalled. If you can name a modern team in pro rugby that doesn't have at least one dominant Pacific Islander as part of that squad, then you're probably lying.

Without the pro game, many of those Pacific Island players wouldn't have reached external rugby markets and spread the message – especially in countries like Wales, where their impact on the sport has been profound. In the early 2020s, Pacific Island teams such as the Fijian Drua and Moana Pasifika are finally getting to play pro rugby for their own people and get the recognition that they deserve, and it's fantastic for the game. Pro rugby wouldn't be the same without the Pacific Island players.

Decision – Rugby is better in the f'ing modern day

NOT EVERYONE SURVIVES

While most of rugby has grown in the professional era, other areas have shrunk. Some have ceased to exist at all. Rugby's growth geographically and financially hasn't been great for everyone, and in some cases it has been catastrophic. As the search for greater player depth and financial resources increased, rugby turned into Pacman, and many clubs were eaten – plus the ones that survived remained as ghosts. As clubs became regions, provinces and franchises, some of the original identity died out. And while it's sad that some clubs no longer exist, or no longer have the gravitas that they once had, rugby is stronger for it. At the local level, everyone deserves access to rugby, which isn't the case at the professional level – the game simply can't afford it. Professional sport isn't sentimental, and it never has been.

Decision – Rugby is better in the f'ing modern day

BARBARIANS STILL RELEVANT

If there's one team that you'd have expected to cease being relevant in the pro era, it's the Barbarians. A team that once brought the best players together from around the world is now essentially mirrored in virtually every pro team in the world. Yet they remain a marquee attraction. What people don't appreciate about the Barbarians is that it offers an almost unique scenario for the players and coaches that are involved. There's no concern about winning, only entertaining. When players become Barbarians, they're allowed to express a level of freedom on the pitch, and 'off', that they don't get in traditional professional rugby environments. For most players, the Barbarians has always been a highlight of their careers.

Decision – the Barbarians have always been f'ing awesome

THE BRITISH AND IRISH LIONS

The British and Irish Lions were conceived in the very beginning of the amateur era, but still thrive in the pro era. While most individual unions, leagues and clubs are pulling in their own directions to the detriment of all others, the Lions are a rare example of cooperation. The Lions are also unique in rugby in that the continuity in quality of play and level of glamour has never faded. The Lions tours in the 1960s are as treasured today as the most recent tours. Plus, of course, the Lions tour is a massive earner for the nations involved and one of the easiest sells in the whole game. While much of rugby is producing financial turds, the Lions are still laying golden eggs.

Decision – The Lions have always been f'ing awesome

WEATHER CONDITIONS

Rugby is a game that has always been heavily influenced by the conditions that it's played in. But until very late in the professional environment (and the advent of multi-country tournaments), most teams just had to worry about localised weather for the whole season. For example, if you were playing amateur rugby in the west of Ireland, then you only had to worry about 60mph winds and rain that could remove a budget hair-system. But if you're Connacht in the modern era, playing in the URC, you could be losing your wig one week, then getting sunburn on that same bald head in Cape Town just seven days later. The weekly changes in conditions that arise from playing in different hemispheres have been fascinating to watch, plus it has presented a coaching challenge that we simply hadn't seen until the late 2010s.

Decision – Rugby is better in the f'ing modern day

EQUIPMENT

THE BOOTS

Rugby boots have come a long way from the old days. Early rugby boots were suitable for not only playing rugby but walking over minefields. They were heavy, weighing nearly 500g per boot and were principally designed for stability and safety. You could argue that the major change in rugby boot usage came in the 1970s when rugby players started to wear football boots, which were by their very design lighter and had a sharper focus on precision and actual contact with the ball – hence they became the choice of backs, as opposed to forwards. Even up until the mid-1990s, most forwards were still using boots specifically designed for forwards' play. Front-row forwards played with steel toe-capped boots, that finished above the ankle and provided stability over everything else. Some of these boots had studs so long that they not only provided stability but with every step also created access to valuable mineral reserves that were largely unreachable using the drilling technology of the day. Meanwhile, second rows and back-row forwards opted for a slightly lower cut, and lighter boot with less protection in the toe – which arguably led to the greatest forwards' boot ever, the Adidas Flanker.

But there's no doubt that the early 2000s saw the greatest change in rugby boot design, where the transition to the full football boot became the norm. The required increase in mobility for all 15 players meant that 400g boots, with a heavy focus on stability, weren't going to cut it anymore and the day of the sub-250g boot had arrived – which some have attributed to an increase in lower leg injuries in the sport.

Unlike the football boot market, where innovations such as the Predator focused on the outer materials, rugby's innovations have tended to focus on the studs. In a modern boot you can now pick one based on the type of ground you're playing on, the weather, or your style of play. Six, eight or moulded studs give the option to dial up or down the traction and mobility required with many players, even at the amateur level, having a couple of boot options to play around with throughout the season.

But without doubt the greatest innovation in rugby boot design over its recent history has been colour. Pre the mid-1990s, rugby boots were designed with the old Henry T. Ford motto: 'If you want any other colour than black, you can go fuck yourself.' (This may not be an accurate quote, but the sentiment is bang on.) Then out of nowhere, players such as Welsh scrum-half Rupert Moon started wearing white boots, a situation that in Llanelli started rumours of a satanic cult having taken over the town. Now, you can wear whatever colour boots you like, with many players' feet looking like they're jammed into a series of poisonous frogs. As an aside, if you want to see the most weird and wonderful choice of rugby footwear, don't look at professional outside-halves playing at the Rugby World Cup, check out your local team's fifth-choice tighthead. For some reason, lower-level tightheads usually wear weirder boots than Kanye West.

Decision – Rugby is better in the f'ing modern day

GUMSHIELDS

Gumshields are arguably the most important piece of equipment in the whole game. Without one, and with your jaw slamming up into your mouth, you can rapidly look like you've had a three-hour session with the lads who got a confession out of Guy Fawkes. Without a gumshield, the potential damage to your teeth, jaw and perhaps more frighteningly the tip of your tongue, is the stuff of the Saw movie franchise. The author of this book has seen a player slice through their own tongue, and it's perplexing why the use of gumshields isn't mandatory across the global game. If you haven't got one, you shouldn't be allowed to play.

The modern gumshield is a marvel compared to the version available in the 1980s and 1990s. For the uninitiated, using a 'do-it-yourself' gumshield involves placing it into boiling water. Then once the rubber has softened, you place it in your mouth and bite into the rubber, thereby creating a replicated shape of your mouth/teeth. Except with the old gumshields, it didn't soften. In the 1990s, a 'do-it-yourself' gumshield was like biting into the tyre of a monster truck. It meant that many players opted for a private dental mould, executed by a dentist, which was bloody expensive. However, the modern 'do-it-yourself' gumshield is a marvel. After 30 seconds in a cup of hot water it softens quicker than a Custard Cream given the same treatment – the result being a perfectly fitting gumshield for about the same price as a pint of continental lager.

Decision – Rugby is better in the f'ing modern day

THE BALL

At first glance, the rugby ball hasn't changed much since the game's inception. But it has – massively. Up until the mid-1990s, rugby balls were as likely to hurt you as any player on the pitch. In the early days of the game pre-1900, the rugby ball was essentially bits of a pig, sewn into bits of a cow. In the mid-1920s, the materials became thinner, which altered the dynamics of the ball, and by the 1950s, the ball had been reduced in length by two inches. Even in the 1990s, when the game was becoming more professional, rugby balls still had the same suppleness as sheet steel. Which makes Paul Thorburn's kick against Scotland in 1986 even more incredible. At 70 yards-ish, it remains one of the longest goal kicks ever completed. Made even more incredible/unbelievable in that the author of this book, along with his friends Matthew Bowen and Martin

Richards, used to help Paul Thorburn with his kicking when they were small kids. As eight-year-olds we used to collect Thorburn's balls (rugby, nothing sinister) when he was practising his kicking on the Welsh school rugby field in Gowerton. We were doing it in the weeks building up to that kick.

Thankfully, by the early to mid-2000s, balls had developed into the type of shape, weight and suppleness required by the modern game, and the benefits are there for all to see. The banana kick, for instance, would not have been possible with an old Mitre Multiplex. The only time you'd hear the word banana in relation to a Mitre Multiplex is when your family brought you some fruit in hospital while you were having your broken foot fixed. But as with most aspects of rugby, the ball development hasn't stopped. The next stage are balls that contain microchips from which the data can be used to calculate kicking distance for coaches and TV audiences. It then won't be long before microchipped balls are part of the officiating process, with microchips in the balls, and in player's clothing, allowing for measurement of the offside line and forward passes, etc.

Decision – Rugby is better in the f'ing modern day

RUGBY SHIRTS

Whether or not rugby shirts are better now or in the old days depends on many factors. It depends on whether you're a supporter or a player. If you're a player, the technology involved in a modern shirt has largely helped. Narrower fits and more slippery core materials have meant that being tackled has become much more difficult. Back in the 1980s, with baggy, oversized shirts, you could tackle a player who was 15 feet away simply by grabbing on to the excess rugby shirt that was flowing down the back of a player's back. If you look at footage of rugby from the 1970s and 1980s, some players had such long shirts (especially second rows) that it looked like they were wearing cotton wedding dresses and were running towards, or away, from a local church.

Whether you like modern shirts, as a player, also depends on what position you play. If you're a 6ft 3in, 15-stone full-back, there's every likelihood that you look resplendent in a modern rugby shirt. With abs and body fat under 18 per cent, the modern rugby shirt is a flattering garment. If you're a 22-stone prop playing in Pro D2, a modern rugby shirt is not only something that makes you look like you haven't bought any new clothes since you were nine years old, but something that you also have to be aided to get in and out of. If you've ever seen a 20-stone lump trying to get into and out of a modern rugby shirt, it's quite a demeaning process.

Then there are the supporters and their feelings towards modern shirts. As a supporter, a modern shirt not only shows the world who you support, but also your BMI. And while supporters want to show their support for their team, they don't always want to look like a badly made raw sausage. This led to the rise of the retro, looser-fitting, supporters' shirt – which is a genius concept and a much-needed revenue stream for many teams. But we can't mention supporters' rugby shirts without mentioning the cost. Nothing riles up rugby supporters more than the cost of rugby shirts. They are, of course, expensive, but rugby shirts aren't any more expensive than the cost of a soccer shirt, or a shirt in the NFL. Professional teams need money, and shirt sales are part of that revenue stream. If you don't want to buy one, don't. Also, as an aside, why is it that most rugby unions shirts have horizontal stripes and soccer/rugby league shirts have vertical stripes? It's as if a load of the creators of both games met up in the 1900s and decided that all rugby union players should be made to look fatter and play in less-flattering patterns – something that most front-row forwards can do without.

Decision – Rugby shirts have always been f'ing cool

PADDING

In the old days there was no such thing as rugby pads. The only padding you had came from muscle or pies. But with the advent of professionalism came a revolution in rugby protection, and padding became the norm. Now it's very rare to see players not wearing some form of shoulder padding, at all levels in the game. Their use is controversial in some ways as, while there's evidence to suggest they help protect against soft tissue damage, there's little proof that they protect against serious injury – especially when it comes to padded headguards. There's also the potential that wearing padding gives you a sense of feeling bigger and more invisible, which can lead to taking more risks in contact. This is particularly true when looking in the mirror before the game, when padding turns you from an 11-stone winger into the love child of Jonah Lomu and Nemani Nadolo. Padding feels like it has made the game safer, even if only to a small degree. Just look at the NFL, for instance; those guys look like they're ready to wrestle hippos. And if the Americans think it's the correct thing to do, who can argue? They never make the wrong decision, ever, ever, ever, ever, ever.

Decision – Rugby is better in the f'ing modern day

GLOVES

Gloves have always met with derision in rugby – which is weird. There have been a few players who have tried wearing them, only to receive lifelong criticism for doing so. Just look at Andy Goode, for example; he had a magnificent career for club and country, yet still people take the piss out of him for looking like an even paler Michael Jackson. Rugby's attitude to gloves is weird. In the NFL, in the catching positions, gloves are almost mandatory. It may be that in rugby the goal isn't just to catch, but also to pass – the friction created by the gloves does slightly affect a player's ability to release the ball smoothly. Despite the obvious benefits, especially in a game played in mid-winter, rugby at all levels seems unwilling to accept the glove.

Decision – Rugby's decision not to adopt gloves is f'ing baffling

THE PITCH

One of the greatest changes in rugby over recent years has been in the surface on which the game has been played. The first synthetic pitch to be approved by the International Rugby Board (IRB as it was known then) was around 2003. But the first professional game to be played on a synthetic pitch didn't happen until almost a decade later. What was once a sport played on grass has become a game played on a veritable cocktail of green things. First, we had full synthetic pitches, then as the decades progressed we moved on to hybrid, or 3G pitches. The benefits have been massive. Modern synthetic pitches use less water, are easier to maintain and, above all, mean that far fewer matches are cancelled due to inclement weather. Prior to synthetic pitches, many clubs, at both professional and amateur level, had pitches with drainage so poor that you could grow rice commercially throughout the winter months, whereas in recent seasons it's very rare to see standing water on any rugby pitch.

But when it comes to synthetic surfaces, it's not all rainbows. There have been many instances of injuries on synthetic pitches, particularly skin burns. Tackling on some of the early synthetic pitches in shorts left your legs and elbows looking like you'd rolled out of an F1 car. Modern pitches aren't perfect, but they're not far off.

Decision – Rugby is better in the f'ing modern day

GPS

GPS, or Global Positioning Systems, have had a massive impact on rugby in the modern era. If you're unfamiliar with them, it's like the microchip that people put in their pet's neck, but for rugby players. They're usually found tucked into the pouch on the back of a player's shirt, which on occasion makes them look like Richard III. GPS principally measures a player's speed, distance covered and the intensity of that speed and distance, which sounds very positive, and it is. But there have been a few drawbacks. With this data, coaches have been able to define exactly when players have reached their peak on-pitch performance, even though most of the data is collected in training sessions and not actual matches. This data has then been used to calculate when players need replacing on the pitch. It's the reason why virtually all front-row forwards are replaced after 55 minutes at Test level and why we sometimes see players being taken from the pitch even when they appear to still be dominating. It's difficult to argue that GPS hasn't improved the efficiency of rugby, but efficiency often creates less space on the pitch, not more.

Decision – Rugby was better in the f'ing old days

OFFICIALS

REFEREES

Referees have the most difficult job in sport, and rugby referees have the most difficult job in refereeing. Rugby is without doubt one of the most complex sports in the world and there's absolutely nothing that you can do to convince the author of this book otherwise. There's simply too much going on at one moment in time for one person to spot it all. If you're a parent, you'll know how difficult it is to monitor the actions and behaviour of a single child, with two it's even harder, with three it's a fucking nightmare. Rugby is like that, but with 30 massive aggressive infants. Rugby, as a sport, has 5 to 16 players run into a contact situation (a ruck), and expecting one person to monitor the position of the ball and all the players at the same time is like asking someone to punch a flower and then count the pollen.

What's perhaps the cruellest aspect of being a referee is that you're the only individual on the pitch who's not allowed to make a single mistake without major abuse. Full-backs are allowed to knock the ball on, centres are allowed to miss tackles, wings are allowed to put their foot in touch, props are allowed to slip the bind, hookers are allowed to not throw straight, locks are allowed to jump across the 'line', and scrum-halves are allowed to talk absolute shit for 80 minutes straight, without any major fallout – yet referees can't put a foot wrong without someone stating that they're a big fan of onanism.

What's even more bizarre about the way in which modern referees are treated is that refereeing is the best it's ever been. Technology now means that more decisions are made correctly, since the game went pro, than they ever were in the amateur era. TV replays have meant that we now get to scrutinise every decision in granular detail, both on and off the pitch. This is something that simply didn't exist in the amateur era. Yet the assertion is that because those mistakes weren't available to see, they simply didn't happen. It's such a weird way to look at it. Most of the iconic tries from yesteryear simply wouldn't have stood under the gaze of modern officials. You just need to look at the iconic

Barbarians try for a start. If you look at the full clip (showing the phases before the initial break from Phil Bennett), the initial lineout throw from New Zealand doesn't appear straight. JPR Williams then has his head taken off twice, and the final pass is forward. Not to mention the 12 missed tackles in the build-up. If that try happened in the modern day, firstly it wouldn't have stood, and, secondly, half of those players would have their contracts torn up and the defence coach would be off to Japan for a season. Refereeing is better in the modern age, and it's not up for debate.

Decision – Rugby is better in the f'ing modern day, it really, really, really is

REFEREES' PHYSIQUES

Referees look very different in the professional era than they did in the amateur one. In the modern era, referees look like they could model underwear for Giorgio Armani, while in the olden days, when all referees were male, most refs looked like they could model for Wonderbra. There's a staggering visual difference between the old and new referees. If you have a shitty TV, or poor wi-fi, it's very easy to mistake a pro-era referee for a player. Some modern referees look like they could not only play full-back at Test level but also go throat-grab to throat-grab with a Test-level openside flanker.

It was only natural that rugby referees' fitness would follow that of modern players, because they literally have to follow the players. One of the most underrated aspects of a referee's job is that they have to keep up with elite professional athletes for 80 minutes. Okay, you can't expect a referee to run alongside Cheslin Kolbe, but he has to remain within 15 yards at a bare minimum. The other thing that rarely gets brought up with regards to the fitness of refs is that they don't have a replacement ready to come on after 50 minutes. Refs have to do the full 80, and think lucidly, all while knowing that someone on Twitter is going to threaten to set fire to their house after the final whistle.

Decision – Rugby is better in the f'ing modern day

REFEREES AS PERSONALITIES

There was a time when referees were allowed to have personalities in rugby. The removal of referees' personalities is a relatively recent thing. Up until the mid-2010s, referees were encouraged to have a personality. To engage with players. To be witty. To be memorable. There are fantastic examples of referees even in recent memory whose personalities became a vital part of the game. Referees such as Nigel Owens were renowned for their player engagement. They had their own highlight reels. They were as big as the players in some regards, which was fantastic for the game. But for some reason, since the advent of social media, supporters no longer seem to want that. The modern referee has to be a rather sombre presence on the pitch. A Victorian figure. Almost an inverted 'Victorian child', to be heard, but not seen. Rugby has a long heritage of referees with personality, and it's a shame that they're no longer allowed to be as such.

Decision – Rugby was better in the f'ing old days

FEMALE REFEREES

It seems really weird that there was a time when rugby didn't have female referees. Even as recently as a decade ago, Nigel Farage would have had a mild stroke had a woman walked out with a whistle. Sara Cox became the first professional women's referee in 2016-ish. Since then, Hollie Davidson and Joy Neville have become regular officials to the point where their sex/gender isn't even referred too, which is a fantastic situation for rugby to be in. Over the next few decades of rugby, it will seem really weird that female referees weren't even a thing. It will be like trying to imagine the world without the internet, microwaves or Pickled Onion Monster Munch.

Decision – Rugby is better in the f'ing modern day

TMO

The TMO (third match official) has arguably become the most hotly debated subject in rugby. While they have clearly made rugby refereeing far more objective and improved the product, they're still hated for some crazy reason. It's a similar situation to William Peel introducing the first-ever professional police force in the world in 1829. You'd think that people would have appreciated someone trying to improve things on the streets, but no, the general public actually threw stones at them. Which is a similar situation with TMOs, but instead of actual rocks being hurled, insults are lobbed via DMs.

One reason that is often used to criticise the TMO's role is how long it takes to get a decision – which is crazy. At worst, the decision takes a couple of minutes. Where exactly do rugby supporters have to be in such a hurry that they can't spare two minutes? While some supporters do metaphorically hold their breath when waiting for the outcome of a decision, they don't literally have to hold their breath – where every ten-second delay is a difference between life of death. The next time there's a slightly longer than normal TMO decision, just breathe deeply, be calm – everything will be fine. TMOs are a great addition to the game.

Decision – Rugby is better in the f'ing modern day

ASSISTANT REFEREES

The term 'assistant referees' (or linesmen/women as they used to be known) has been one of rugby's more successful rebrands. Prior to this, linesmen/women were largely second-class citizens in the refereeing world. Especially at local level, where to make them look even more like a sub-species they often didn't have a flag to wave, but instead had to make do with a ten-year-old Umbro hoody riddled with holes. But it's more than just the name that has elevated the role of the assistant referee. Their responsibilities on the pitch have also broadened and their ability to interject and help with decision-making has been a massive plus. No greater example of this promotion for assistant referees can be found than their input into the interpretation of dangerous tackles. Those decisions are very difficult to get right as an individual, and having a circle of additional decision-makers certainly helps. It also spreads the inevitable abuse on social media between the three of you, not just one.

Decision – Rugby is better in the f'ing modern day

TREATMENT OF OFFICIALS ON SOCIAL MEDIA

The treatment of officials on social media has been touched on in the previous passages, but it's deserving of its own section. Rugby has moved forwards in so many ways. But one way in which it has gone backwards is in the treatment of officials by supporters. The treatment that referees now have to tolerate is ridiculous, leaving many to actually retire early or just leave the game entirely. As was mentioned previously, referees are the only people on the pitch who get absolutely vilified for one mistake, yet a player can make three and walk away largely unscathed on social media. Being able to criticise a referee for a mistake is one thing, sending them death threats is quite another. If you're one of those people who has sent death threats or abusive messages to a referee, then the author of this book hopes that you somehow swallow a dried pea and end up accidentally whistling every time you breathe for the rest of your life.

Decision – Rugby was better in the f'ing old days

TECHNOLOGY IN REFEREEING

Despite its image of crusty old men in blazers and ties, eating albino swan sandwiches from a plate shaped from the ground-up beaks of the remaining dodos (which are bred at the Illuminati's official zoo in Geneva), the sport as a whole is very progressive when it comes to laws and technology. But weirdly it isn't when it comes to the actual kit that the referee has on their person. It seems weird that in a game that tracks the movement of each player via GPS and has a chip inside the ball that can measure its movement, offsides and forward passes aren't immediately calculated – at elite level, of course. The author of this book isn't suggesting that Gowerton RFC should invest in £50k's worth of new GPS kit – Steve Howells and Chunky wouldn't allow it (and Richard Edwards would mock it); they run a tight, brilliant ship down there. But at elite level it seems as if some of the game's most controversial decisions could be eliminated overnight with a simple app for the ref and the kit that already exists in the ball and the players' jerseys. Get it sorted, someone.

Decision – Rugby will hopefully be even f'ing better in the future

SAFETY

HEAD INJURY ASSESSMENTS (HIAS)

The term head injury in rugby has changed more than the meaning of arguably any other word. Head injury used to mean a cut to your cheek from a stray stud, or a black eye from a punch. It used to mean injuries that healed in a couple of days or weeks. They were injuries that you largely wore as a badge of honour from making a tackle. Now it means something far more serious. The term head injury means long-term health problems that don't disappear and can't be sorted out with a few stitches.

Since the game has gone professional (especially since early 2010), head injuries have finally received the awareness they deserve, and the attention. Some will still argue that head injuries, in their modern definition, are just a part of the game, and if you don't want to get a concussion, then don't play. This attitude is almost unique to players and supporters who grew up watching the game in the 1980s and earlier – when backs, especially, were small enough to be carried on to a plane as hand luggage. Thankfully, now, rugby has a very secure procedure for catching head injuries on the pitch – something that would have been laughed at about 30 years ago. Perhaps the greatest change that's happened in the modern game is the realisation that a player's health is more important than the result – that isn't an attitude that prevailed until very recently. Rugby used to have a very aggressive approach to injuries, whereby playing on with an injury was seen as a sign of strength and masculinity – now it's seen as a sign of stupidity, and rightly so.

Decision – Rugby is better in the f'ing modern day

GOUGING

Gouging has never been in fashion, or vogue. It has always been an act perpetrated by absolute shithouses. The only saving grace for rugby is that modern technology has made it far easier to spot and punish. In most modern cases of gouging, the instances have been largely accidental, which still isn't great, but it's still far better than the old days where some players would try to remove your eyeball, like a crow pecking at an abandoned lamb in a field.

Decision – Rugby is better in the f'ing modern day

FIGHTING

Rugby has a weird relationship with fighting. It's the same as most people's relationship with McDonald's – in that we all love it, but have to deny it in public. There's not a single supporter in the game who upon seeing a fight wants it to stop for any reason other than the possibility of their team conceding a penalty or a card. In the amateur era, fighting was a part of the game. In fact, it was a legit part of the game. It wasn't even just something that affected open play, or the breakdown. Many kick-offs/restarts in the old days resulted in some fight or another. Back then players weren't checking their position in relation to the ball in the air, they were checking their position in relation to the opposition's flying elbows.

Prior to the influence of TV and replays, most fights weren't even spotted by officials. Most violent incidents were treated like the bareknuckle boxing scene, in that you knew it was happening, but very little was done about it. As a result, fighting often went unpunished entirely. Even the fights that were spotted were solved not with yellow or red cards, but with forced anaemic handshakes. It's easy to see why rugby had to relinquish its love of fighting. Much like ice hockey, the optics for legal violence within a sport's law book aren't great. Especially when you're trying to attract younger players and sponsors – there are very few brand managers in the commercial world looking to sponsor a sport whose brand values include a desire to batter someone in the face. Fighting is rugby's alcohol, in that while we all realise that we have to cut down on our drinking, many of us like a swig of it now and again – rugby also literally has the vice of alcohol, of course, which is a separate subject entirely.

Decision – Rugby was better in the f'ing old days

RUCKING

Rucking is the corporal punishment/national conscription of rugby, in that a lot of older people liked it, and despite its perceived effectiveness, it's fucking horrific. Rucking, for those readers who are under the age of 40, was when players were allowed to 'remove you' from the ruck with their feet (if you were on the wrong side of the ball). It was like having the conveyor belt at Lidl roll over your body – if that conveyor belt were covered in varying degrees of sharpened metal. Players were broadly only allowed to 'ruck' on your legs and back, but it still hurt. Especially after the game, when you were playing youth rugby and your mother insisted on tipping Dettol into your post-match bath. If you're still struggling to picture the scenario, imagine a player being fed feet-first into a low-quality combine harvester.

However, with rucking there was no jackaling – which is arguably a far more dangerous enterprise. You simply wouldn't stand there and try to win the ball with eight players polishing their studs on your spine. The resulting stripes on your back, when playing with rucking, meant that most players looked like they'd run through Whipsnade lions' enclosure, naked, covered in zebra blood, shouting, 'You lions are absolute shithouses.' A few stripes on your back are obviously far more desirable than the repeated concussion and spinal damage created by being cleaned out in the jackal. However, it would be naive to assume that rucking only took place on players' legs and backs. When things got nasty, it would often happen to someone's head and the injuries would be horrific. Rucking did keep some people in line and prevented other forms of skulduggery, but you could say the same about the Kray twins, and no one wants those lunatics back in society.

Decision – Rugby is like Switzerland when it comes to rucking, and the decision shall remain neutral

STAMPING

Similar to rucking (as above) but with more downward force. Whereas rucking was designed to remove players from the wrong side of the ball, stamping removed players from the rugby pitch and into ambulances. Stamping never had a place in rugby and was always a coward's trick. It was then, as it is now, only something executed by your team's absolute idiot – the player that no one really likes. Players who stamped like to be known as 'hard' but were actually mostly just hard-of-thinking.

Decision – Rugby is better in the f'ing modern day

SPONGES

Sponges still exist in rugby because some things still need wiping. But sponges are no longer like they were in the old days. In the old days, sponges were the only pieces of medical equipment available at all levels of the game. If you had a cut, you got the sponge. If you snapped both ankles, you got the sponge. If your head was pulled off, a sponge was then placed upon your shoulders to create the façade of a head. It didn't matter what level you played at, the only thing that tended to change with regards to sponge usage was the temperature of the water – cold for some injuries, warm for others. Though the reasons for using cold water on some injuries and warm on others were never fully disclosed. If your kitman had any kind of sprays or lotions, in the old days, he was regarded as a magician or some kind of warlock and often not trusted by the village elders.

Looking back, what's truly amazing is that sponges didn't kill more people in rugby. While we regard scrummaging, high tackles and gouging as dangerous within the sport, they're nothing compared to the concoction of germs that could be found on the sponge itself or bubbling at the bottom of the cracked bucket – the bucket is where the sponge lived on weekdays. If someone told the author of this book that Covid initially came from a rugby sponge in 1976, it would come as no surprise – and could possibly have led to the quicker discovery of a vaccine and negated the pandemic.

Decision – Rugby is better in the f'ing modern day

SAFETY ON THE BUS

Rugby and its safety levels on the pitch have increased enormously. But safety levels on the way to and from the game also seem to have improved, especially at the amateur level. There was a time in the 1980s and 1990s, where some of the 'acts' that occurred on rugby buses ranged from the stupid to the illegal. One youth team in South Wales (that the author of this book knows of) used to regularly strip the new youth players of their clothes, kick them off the bus, then leave them no choice but to run all the way back to the clubhouse – which was about a mile away from the 'forced' drop-off point. To get back to the clubhouse, it meant running up towards the top of the village, off the main road, hopping through various gardens and hoping that you found some washing on a line that you could use to cover yourself. This practice was stopped in about 1994 when, legend has it, the mayor of Swansea was travelling through the village, on official business, and saw a pasty white thing running for its life.

But by far and away the worst game the author has ever heard about on a rugby bus was 'Freckles' – do not read this if you're squeamish or ever want to eat food again. 'Freckles' is a game so weird that it wouldn't even feature on *Squid Game*. If fact, if you asked most of the contestants on *Squid Game* whether they'd rather play 'Freckles' or take a bullet in the face from that giant creepy doll thing, they'd take the bullet. 'Freckles' involved sitting on the only seats on the bus that had a table in the centre, usually four of you, each with a can of lager. Then everyone had to put their face down on the edge of the table. With four of you, now with your chins resting down low, mouth firmly closed, someone defecates in the middle of the table. Yup that's right, you read that correctly. All that then remains is for a can of lager to be dropped on to the lump of brown stuff and for whoever has the most 'freckles' on their face to drink their can of lager – I did warn you that it was bad.

Ralgex and Deep Heat spray were also the weapons of rugby's torturers during this period. The number of players who will have spent Saturday evening with a stinging sensation around certain parts of their body during the 1980s and 1990s would number in the thousands. What was perhaps funnier to the onlookers wasn't that amusing to the victim, when the victim was strolling around Swansea city centre on a Saturday evening with a scrotum warm enough to sear a tomahawk steak. Anecdotally, and thankfully, rugby seems to have calmed down a lot since the 1990s. As a player who was involved in youth rugby during this period, the author of this book dreaded the bus ride home, especially during my first season. For that reason, rugby and its bus trips seem to be in a far better place.

Decision – Rugby is better in the f'ing modern day

MONEY

PLAYER WAGES

All sports have a line-in-the-sand moment. In union it occurred in 1996. But in the wider, earlier days of the sport of rugby it happened back in the late 19th century. In the late 1880s, it was forbidden to be paid to play rugby, which was initially a public-school game. But as the game became a bigger draw in working-class cities (mostly up north), players couldn't afford to not work on a Saturday, hence they were paid, hence the split. But we digress; 1996 was the year that union officially went pro, but as we all know it was happening a long time before that. Prior to 1996, rugby union players were often given preferable terms for jobs instead of money, or cash used to magically appear in their boots – sometimes brand-new cars would appear on their drives – via the rugby fairy. All of which is totally justified. Why should people have played for free, when the clubs/unions surrounding them were profiting?

However, while players obviously have the right to be paid in the professional game, since 1996 rugby's finances have never really balanced. You could argue that union has always been all fur coats and no knickers since its very inception. Rugby clubs rarely break even and often operate at a loss. Even the biggest unions, with complete domination over their local sporting markets, struggle to run as legit going concerns. The situation has, of course, got worse since the pandemic of 2020. If there was ever a sport that was living pay cheque to pay cheque, it was rugby union. And when the pay cheque stopped coming, multiple clubs went under – namely in the English Premiership. Rugby union is a niche sport, and one that will always be so – it's way too complicated for mainstream viewers. Whether money in rugby has benefited the sport is not up for question. Having professional players, training all day and focusing on rugby as their job has improved the game beyond any recognition. Whether the sport should be paying as much as it does, when it clearly can't afford to, is not so clear.

Decision – Rugby never has known what to do when it comes to f'ing money

WAGES PER POSITION

As we have discussed, money for rugby players is a must. If you want a professional product, you need to pay for it. But not all players get the same wedge, and you'd be surprised how much it varies by position. You may also be surprised to learn that it varies by league, with the Top 14, for example, having higher wages in the tight five than some other leagues. But if we use the English Premiership as an example, it provides a good breakdown of the rough difference. Top of the earners are, of course, outside-halves, which is why they can afford such expensive haircuts. Even though the creative role of an outside-half has arguably diminished, the need for accurate kicking has not – hence the expense. At the other end of the scale, and perhaps most cruelly (as they stand next to each other), is the scrum-half. Scrum-halves are the lowest-paid in most teams, which is a contributory factor as to why they're so angry all the time. Back-row forwards always tend to be in the top third of the list, largely due to the attritional nature of the role; they are, after all, the front-line infantry of rugby and the ones who quite literally and metaphorically get repeatedly sent over the top.

Perhaps the greatest surprise to many when looking at the wages of players is at lock. Many seem to think that locks are the lanky bumbling land mammals of rugby – merely hitting rucks and doing a bit of jumping. But that notion couldn't be further from the truth. Locks are among the rarest of players, especially Test-quality locks. The reality is that in the men's game in particular, the global population simply doesn't have that many people who have the physique to play the position. The sifting process for locks is very narrow and precise – especially in the men's game. Firstly, you need people who are 6ft 6in tall – minimum. They must be 17 stone – minimum. Then once you've found this rare bunch, they must also like getting hurt, while cleaning out 25 attacking rucks per game and enjoy grabbing other people's throats. Of course, the very best locks in the world hover even above this ridiculous list of requirements. Think Eben Etzebeth, RG Snyman, Will Skelton, etc. They are 6ft 8in-plus and weigh more than most married couples. You simply don't see people of this size wandering around the streets, especially if you live in a country with a small population. If you see a man who's 6ft 9in tall in Cardiff city centre, it's a big deal and you assume that someone from the *Guinness Book of Records* will shortly arrive and catch them with a butterfly net. Whereas in South Africa, you'll probably see three blokes over 6ft 9in tall standing in the queue at the local petrol station.

It's a very similar situation with tighthead props, as opposed to loosehead props. Often their average wage is added together, giving a misleading result, because tighthead props often earn far more. In the Top 14, for instance, tighthead props tend to be the highest earners, simply because there aren't that many people who can run while simultaneously being as difficult to move as an eight-yard builder's skip. There may not be enough money in professional rugby to cover these salaries long-term, globally. But it's hard to ignore the fact that modern players have improved as a result.

Decision – Rugby is better in the f'ing modern day

COST OF TICKETS

The cost of rugby tickets is something that will, and has always, annoyed supporters. But it shouldn't. Seeing cool things costs money. Seeing cool amateur things used to cost money. Seeing professional things costs more. Sports fans always seem to have issues with paying for tickets, regardless of the sport. And rugby is no different. The biggest criticism of rugby tickets is usually saved for Test rugby, where tickets can cost £100-plus. But the reality is that those tickets, by and large, sell. Despite what most fans think, ticket prices aren't just decided in a rugby boardroom where chimpanzees throw darts at various prices on the wall. Ticket prices are priced to sell at the optimum price, and it has always been that way. The other cruel truth is that you don't have to pay that much for a rugby ticket if you don't want to – you don't have to go at all. But without doubt the most irritating part of supporters complaining about the ticket process is that in the next breath they'll also say there's no money in rugby and that their team can't afford to compete. Professional rugby costs money and the hard truth is that supporters like us have to pay for it.

Decision – Rugby is better in the f'ing modern day

COST OF RUGBY SHIRTS

As above, the cost of rugby shirts is one of rugby's major seasonal bugbears. It's a great example of rugby retaining its amateur ethos when it comes to money in the sport. Most rugby supporters still think that you should be able to buy rugby shirts when you're

18 years of age and then not have to buy another one ever again – unless you want to be buried in a fresh one. The fact that rugby clubs tend to release new shirts every season is often only matched in negative public reaction by a major increase in taxation from central government. Few supporters appreciate that new shirts are a key revenue stream for their club or country. Most supporters will go mental when having to spend £70 on a rugby top, yet quite happily buy six pints of expensive Italian lager and a curry for the same total – the rugby shirts last a lot longer. Pro rugby costs money and it's got to be paid for somehow.

Decision – Rugby is better in the f'ing modern day

PAYMENTS IN AMATEUR RUGBY

Saying 'payments in amateur rugby' is mental. It is a dichotomy from the get-go. There should be no payments in amateur rugby to players – at all. But they do still happen. Everyone reading this book who's part of an amateur rugby club will know of a team paying some of their players. It's the scourge of the amateur game and a contributing factor to the financial problems in the professional game – this only relates to player payments, not payments to support the wider grassroots development. Perhaps the greatest hypocrisy of the amateur game is that you'll often hear someone at the amateur end of the sport criticise pro rugby for being 'all about money', while at the same time poaching players from a nearby rival with the odd £100 here and there. Professional rugby has many problems keeping its finances in check, but the same issues apply in the amateur game. And in some ways it's more serious, as money should have nothing to do with player retention at the amateur level.

Decision – Can someone please stop amateur rugby teams paying f'ing players

SPONSORSHIP

Sponsorship is as much a part of rugby as losing to New Zealand. It's a massive revenue channel for both the professional and amateur game, yet it continues to be a stick with which the old amateur ethos beats the pro ethos. For some reason, those from the old school don't mind having sponsors on the programmes, they don't mind sponsors on the side hoardings, they don't mind sponsors on TV content, but if you place a sponsor on the middle of a shirt or, heaven forbid, rename a stadium, all hell breaks loose.

It's incredible to think that the All Blacks have only really started having shirt sponsors in the last decade (the ABs flirted with sponsorship in the late 1990s but only went hardcore with it in the last decade). Yet when they did, it was met with the same type of response you'd expect if you invited some New Zealanders around for Sunday lunch and presented them with roasted kiwi – with all the trimmings. But if there's one element of sponsorship that still manages to smoke even the most unlikely of rugby's 'gammons', then it's the renaming of stadiums with that of a sponsor. If you dare to rename a stadium, it's as if you've decided to rename your children 'Pissflap' and 'Spunkbomb'. All levels of rugby need sponsorship, and pro rugby really needs it.

Decision – Rugby is better in the f'ing modern day

SALARY CAPS

Salary caps are where all teams, in a given league, agree not to spend over a certain budget. It's designed to promote fairness and longevity in those leagues. But as we know, even when those salary caps have been signed, there's often the use of invisible ink. There is, of course, an argument for a salary cap in all individual leagues, otherwise those teams with more resources become dominant to the point where competition ceases to exist. But there's arguably a greater argument for rugby to have a salary gap across all leagues – especially leagues in the same locality. It will never happen, of course, as certain leagues have better financing than others. But, as a rule, the constant demand for higher wages in some leagues will always put pressure on the rest – with consolidation of teams or total collapse being the outcome. While the amateur age of rugby wasn't ideal, it did at least mean that every league was largely running on the same salary cap – nothing. In regards to the fairness across the whole sport, not paying at all was the greatest salary cap in the history of the game.

Decision – Rugby never has known what to do when it comes to f'ing money

COACHING

Coaching has undergone an evolution so rapid that it would have made Charles Darwin shit his pants. To a casual supporter, the game from the 1970s probably looks similar to the game in 2025, but to those who watch regularly it looks like a very different sport. Where rugby once seemed to have enough space on the pitch to graze a sizeable herd, it now has less space than a studio flat in Yokohama. Back then, defence was largely an ad hoc affair, with 'numbering up' being the main consideration, and much of a coach's job was motivation. But that's no longer the case. Modern rugby is no longer a game where space is allowed to exist for more than 0.3345 of a second. The sport now measures 'gaps' in centimetres, not metres. If you don't read a modern coaching manual every three years, then much of your rugby knowledge is largely debunked after that period has elapsed. Professional rugby coaching is a far more accurate discipline than that of its amateur era.

Decision – Rugby is better in the f'ing modern day

NUMBER OF COACHES

The term 'rugby coaches' has become an increasingly accurate term, in that you now need a large bus just to get the coaching staff to the match. The number of coaches involved in rugby is now absolutely incredible – with many professional teams having more coaches than amateur teams had players. The increase in the number of coaches has followed the increase in the required detail involved in the game. In a sport where the ruck, maul, scrum, lineout and restart are all essentially mini-sports within a larger sport, each requires a level of detail that only watch repairers can truly appreciate. There is absolutely no doubt that the number of coaches involved in the modern game has improved the sport.

Decision – Rugby is better in the f'ing modern day

COACHING TERMINOLOGY

As a sport, rugby probably creates more additional words per season than Shakespeare did in his entire career. 'Pods' were once the sole domain of dolphins, peas and vanilla, but now they are central to any conversation around rugby and its structures. If you thought that 'jackals' were carnivorous creatures, then you'll be super confused when you see that the best tend to be under six foot and have just two legs. Then there are instances where rugby delves into the realm of Pythagoras and starts using phrases like 'above the horizontal', or flirts with the use of DIY words like 'hinging'. If you don't keep up with rugby's new vocab, you're going to end up like one of those Tory MPs who thinks that people still value Latin. The game has changed rapidly and its dictionary has had to follow.

Decision – Rugby has always used complicated f'ing language

LAPTOPS AND SPREADSHEETS

Laptops and spreadsheets were once the domain of accountants, project managers and drug dealers who had an attention to detail that was ahead of their time.

But in the modern era, no rugby coach can be without one. Most rugby coaches have closer relationships with their laptop, than they do their own family's pet – some coaches walk their laptops on Sunday mornings. To many coaches, the whole game is viewed through the prism of the laptop – even though the game is happening live in front of them. With data being so important to the modern game, it's understandable that many of the coaching team have to live code during the match – but it still looks a bit weird. Also, while modern society is worrying about the amount of time that kids spend on devices, no one is showing the same level of concern for rugby coaches and their laptops – it's a concern and deserves its own pressure group.

Decision – Rugby was better in the f'ing old days

STRENGTH AND CONDITIONING

Money is, of course, the best tool with which to differentiate rugby from the amateur and pro eras of the game. But the other is strength and conditioning (S+C). In the amateur era, rugby players looked like the normal people on the street. They were, of course, fitter than the general population, but if you saw a Test-level forward wandering around your local city centre in 1970, they wouldn't look much different to your mates. These days, if you see a Test-level forward wandering around your local city centre, they look like they could put you and all your mates in one big pile, deadlift the lot of you and then eat you. This isn't to say that players in the 1970s and 80s weren't strong, they obviously were. But it tended to be strength derived from their jobs at the time – functional strength. In Wales, for instance, many of the best front-row forwards from that era were farmers. And while they were only 14 or 15 stone in weight (some even less) they were literally moving livestock around all day. If you can lift 15 sheep off their feet every hour, you can do the same to most humans for 80 minutes.

Although, while S+C has obviously improved, one aspect of the pre-game S+C that the author of this book still can't get his head around, is why the pre-match warm-up is so intense. If props can only play for 55 minutes during the match, why are they absolutely thrashed for 30 minutes before it? Many modern players wander into the changing rooms before the match (after the warm-up) in the same condition that most players in the amateur era seemed to enter the changing rooms after the match. However, when push literally comes to shove, there's no denying that modern players are far fitter and stronger.

Decision – Rugby is better in the f'ing modern day

INNOVATION

Coaches used to be judged by wins and trophies. But for the modern coach that's no longer enough. Many of the best modern coaches are now known for innovation, and that is often how their legacy is judged. They look to create some coachable aspects of rugby that are uniquely identifiable to them. Rassie Erasmus is a great case in point. Erasmus is the bonkers scientist of rugby, and he has been great for the game. His innovation with bench selection (the 6:2 split), the 'traffic lights' and, of course, becoming 'the waterboy' have genuinely changed the game and are now being copied by others. Erasmus's innovations are arguably as influential in rugby as Pep Guardiola's have been in European soccer. Results are no longer enough for the modern coach; innovation is where it's at.

Decision – Rugby is better in the f'ing modern day

OLD-SCHOOL VS NEW-SCHOOL ATTITUDES

The separation between old-school and new-school managers is stark. If you run a list of coaches from the last 40 years through your imagination, it's easy to split them into the old vs new category. The separation isn't usually done by the actual coaching itself, but how it's delivered. There are those who shout, scream and motivate largely through fear, and those who do it via conversation, reinforcement and encouragement. It may seem like a rather unnecessary distinction to make, but it does matter, and for one major reason: players no longer respond to the old-school. Yes, every player needs a talking-to on occasions (much like any other job), but screaming and bawling rarely works long-term.

The old-school coaches are usually easy to spot. They deliver big increases in performance initially, but then it drops off after about 18 months – when players simply stop responding to getting bollocked. The new-school coaches often have slower starts, performance-wise, but tend to deliver over longer periods. As much as rugby has tended to glorify the shouty coach in the past, the only place for hairdryers in the modern changing room is on the wall – for outside-halves to use after they shower their delicate bodies.

Decision – Rugby is better in the f'ing modern day

DIVERSITY

WOMEN'S RUGBY

Women have played rugby for a long time. Women have played Test rugby for the last 40-ish years. But only in the last decade have things really changed. Prior to that, women's rugby was treated like men's netball – it's probably happening somewhere, but no one really gives a shit. That's no longer the case. Women's rugby is now part of the mainstream discussion and, while it's still some way behind getting parity in terms of media coverage, it is hugely visible in rugby media. Women's rugby is slowly following the financial path of men's rugby in the mid-1990s in that some nations and teams are further ahead than others, which creates a huge disparity in not just financial terms but also in results. This will hopefully change as the game gains more traction over the coming decades. Many judge whether women's rugby is currently delivering the same impact as men's rugby, which is impatient and unfair. Women's rugby has only been professional (since the time of writing this book) for half a decade-ish. As a sport, women's rugby shouldn't be judged financially on this generation, but in two generations time, when those generations of girls have had access to the game and exposure to rugby media.

Decision – Rugby is better in the f'ing modern day

WHEELCHAIR RUGBY

Wheelchair rugby is mental. This might seem like a politically incorrect statement, but it isn't. Wheelchair rugby is arguably the most aggressive version of the sport. It's a cross between crashing a car and playing rugby. Again, this might seem insensitive. Until you consider that when one wheelchair rugby player was asked, 'Why is the game so violent?' he replied, 'I'm already in a wheelchair, what's the worst that can happen?' If you've never seen a game of wheelchair rugby, then do. It makes 15-a-side look like a gathering of pacifists.

Decision – Rugby is better in the f'ing modern day

THE TRANSGENDER ISSUE

The game for all shapes and sizes has met its end level boss with the subject of transgender players in rugby. There's seemingly no easy solution to the problem. The discussion on both sides can become very intense very quickly and has led to the topic largely being shouted, rather than discussed. Rugby has taken many years to ease its issues with sexism, racism and homophobia. How it handles the transgender issue remains to be seen. At the time of writing this book, in 2025, it looks as though transgender athletes will have to play with the sex that they were born with.

Decision – Rugby genuinely doesn't seem to know what the f'ing answer is

GAY PLAYERS

There's no use saying that rugby didn't used to be homophobic in the amateur era. It did. And it was openly so. In the 1990s, the pejorative homophobic language used in rugby was widespread – it was almost a given. Calling someone a 'gaylord' or saying 'shut up, you bender' was par for the course – a horrible shameful course. But now that has thankfully changed. Or at least through the prism of the white straight bloke who has written this book it has – the reality may still be very different if you're a gay player or supporter.

A major turning point in the game was undoubtedly when Gareth Thomas 'came out'. Thomas undid the stereotype of a gay man in about 20 minutes – given that he was one of the most ruthless, hardest players to play the game in Wales. Even since Thomas made the first move for gay male players in rugby, things seem to have progressed considerably. The same can be said for women's rugby, where rarely are players' sexual preferences ever referenced anymore – which simply wouldn't have been the case in the amateur era. The sport now also has various teams across the globe who are openly gay, or gay-focused, which is something that seemed like a pipe dream even in the early 2000s. Rugby still has a long way to go when it comes to homophobia, but it has made some vital metres.

Decision – Rugby is better in the f'ing modern day

RACE

While rugby has always presented itself as a game for all shapes and sizes, that hasn't always been the case when it comes to colour. Rugby's issues with racism have swung from the casual to the outright criminal – the South African issue being a stain that has taken many years to remove from the game. Growing up watching rugby in the 1980s, and beyond, rugby was a white sport in virtually all countries, not just South Africa. If you had to pick one moment where things changed, it was the 1995 Rugby World Cup in South Africa. From the moment that Chester Williams played for the Springboks, and Nelson Mandela became part of the celebrations, it felt like rugby was going to move forwards – and it did. Teams that were once all white now have very visible representation from many ethnicities. Racism is still evident in rugby, but it has taken big steps forwards.

Decision – Rugby is better in the f'ing modern day

OVERALL ACCEPTANCE

Overall, rugby seems to be a more welcoming place than it was in the amateur era. Many will argue that it was always welcoming, and it was – if you were white, male and straight. Anecdotally, the average local rugby club that the author of this book frequents is a very different place to those that he visited as a younger man. Most clubs now have thriving junior sections, women's teams and the clubhouse is a place where women are openly drinking in the bar, not merely serving behind it. The attendances at modern rugby matches are also notably more mixed with regards to sex, race and most other metrics. Rugby needs to keep moving forwards, and currently it is.

Decision – Rugby is better in the f'ing modern day

MATCHDAY EXPERIENCE

DRINKS AT THE RUGBY

Drinks at the rugby have come a long way. That is if any of the rugby purists will let you buy more than two pints. According to rugby purists, if you queue for beer and drink it during the game, then you don't understand rugby and want the game to fail. But if you do manage to sneak away from a rugby purist to grab a drink, then the options are far more varied than they were in the old days. In the 1980s you had one choice, beer. Often there was a single choice of beer from the local brewery, which was of questionable quality and often had bits of stuff floating around in it. But bits floating around in your beer didn't really matter back then because most people were either working in mines or had their hands stuck in cotton looms – so any pint seemed like heaven. Also, if you were a woman at the rugby, who back then were only allowed to drink wine or sherry for some reason, then you had to either have water or nothing.

The above is, of course, hyperbole, but it does reflect the old matchday experience. Now, it has the same range of drinks as your local bar, and it's awesome. Plus, some stadiums have those machines that appear from underground and fill four pints in one go through magic holes in the bottom of the glass. If those four-pint magic-machines don't impress you, then this book may not be for you.

Decision – Rugby is better in the f'ing modern day

DRUNKS AT THE RUGBY

Neatly linking to the above paragraph is the question of people drinking too much at the rugby. This subject once again seems to link in with the rugby snobbery movement – those people who simply don't like to see people having fun at the rugby. Over the past decade or so, certain aspects of the rugby media have started suggesting that there's a massive alcohol problem at rugby matches – especially at Test matches. Many media outlets would have you believe that modern stadiums on matchday become gin-soaked vomit shacks, the sort you'd have found in the Victorian East End. But the author of this book has genuinely never seen this happen. Yes, there are pissed people at the rugby, and booze is everywhere, but it's by no means a worry or any different to any other area of sports entertainment. Have you ever seen the crowds at the tennis in the US Open, at the golf, or at the racing – where some punters drink so much at some races that they actually piss more, collectively, than the horses. Rugby has no bigger problem with alcohol than any other area of sports entertainment.

Decision – Rugby has always like a f'ing pint

FOOD AT THE RUGBY

Food at the rugby has improved hugely. Largely because until about ten years ago 'eating was cheating', and anyone (man or woman) found eating while being out at the rugby on an 'all-dayer' was deemed to be an embarrassment to their parents. Thankfully that's no longer the case and people no longer have to pretend that their digestive system shuts down while having a day at the rugby and do actually need food to continue living. The food revolution at the rugby has been noticeable and has stopped the next generation of rugby supporters believing that the only food available at rugby was chips or what can loosely be described as shaped meats. In the 1980s and 1990s, food at the rugby seemed to involve chips and weirdly shaped lumps of protein that sat in what appeared to be shallow pools of warm water. This meat and chips was then put in a bread roll that looked like it hadn't been cut with a knife, but instead divided into two by a pissed-up woodpecker. Since then, the 'pop-up' food stall has revolutionised food and meant that rugby supporters can now eat the same food as those normal people in wider society.

Decision – Rugby is better in the f'ing modern day

PEOPLE STANDING UP

Apparently, in recent decades, rugby has had a massive problem with people standing up at the match and blocking other people's views. It's a really weird criticism to make of rugby that people are now standing up and blocking views, because unlike in the old days virtually no one is standing up. In the old days, virtually everyone was standing. For some reason, modern fans can't have their view blocked for even 2.3 seconds while watching the rugby. And if they have to stand up for 1.3 seconds, then their entire day is ruined, possibly their week. Some find having to stand up twice in 80 minutes for someone to pass by so unbearable that they take to social media and say that they'll never watch rugby again. Perhaps the weirdest aspect is that most supporters are expecting their team and players to go out and risk everything for 80 minutes, make 30 tackles, carry for 80 metres, yet can't lift their buttocks 18 inches and let someone pass by to take a piss.

Decision – Rugby has always had people f'ing standing up and moving about

TOILETS

When someone in their 70s tells you watching rugby in stadiums was better in the 1980s, remind them that most toilets in stadiums back then had a solid inch of piss on the floor. Unlike most of this book, the above isn't hyperbole. In the 1980s, in the old national stadium in Wales, the whole toilet area would have a solid inch of piss on the floor. As a young boy, the author of this book would regularly have urine pour over the top of his shoes in the toilets. Back then, in most grounds, men used to piss in sinks, on walls or just in the corridor – there was literally piss everywhere. The number of toilets was so insufficient that it was like watching rugby in the middle of the Nile – if the Nile was tinged yellow and stank of Brains SA. When people tell you watching rugby was better in the old days, just think of a seven-year-old boy watching Neath vs Swansea in the Schweppes Cup Final, with enough piss on his socks to tan the hides of 15 American buffalo.

Decision – Rugby is better in the f'ing modern day

MUSIC AT THE RUGBY

We touched on music at the rugby in the 'rugby snobs' section. So, we won't go into too much detail here. Suffice to say that music is usually a pretty good idea at the rugby, otherwise you have to listen to gangs of old men wittering on about how rugby isn't the same as it used to be. I'd rather listen to 80 minutes of German Gabba than listen to those guys.

Decision – Rugby is better in the f'ing modern day

PROGRAMMES

On the decline and just as difficult to chew, the printed rugby programme is the dodo of rugby publications. Rugby programmes used to be a given on a matchday. It was part of the matchday experience. It was like the ticket's sibling – they just came together. But sadly no longer. The rise of digital media and a decrease in the use of paper has meant that the paper programme is rather an atavistic remnant of rugby. It's a shame, as rugby programmes are almost a living record of rugby history. They're the paper Wikipedia of rugby, in that virtually every major game that has ever taken place came with a programme. You can, of course, get a digital copy to download on to your phone or tablet. But it just feels wrong. It's like making a roast dinner in an air fryer.

Decision – Rugby was better in the f'ing old days

STADIUMS

Stadiums in the modern day are far better than they were in the old days. And if you don't agree, there's something wrong with you. Most old stadiums had 'standing' in the majority of the stadium. Standing is shit. If standing was great, we wouldn't have chairs and DFS wouldn't be having a f'ing sale every week. Standing without a roof over your head was even shitter. Weirdly, in some old stadiums it was better to be standing without any roof over your head, than standing near the edge of the roof. If you were unlucky enough to be standing within three feet of a roof's edge, you'd often have sheets or water flowing off the roof, directly on to your head and down the back of your neck. You'd have so much water dropping on you from a height that it looked like you were in some kind of shampoo advert – but set in f'ing Llanelli.

Decision – Rugby is better in the f'ing modern day

MASCOTS

Mascots are weird things in rugby and, of course, a relatively new invention. Most mascots are there to appeal to children but actually tend to scare the author of this book. Mascots are not animals, nor humans – they live in a unique mascot realm. They also tend to communicate entirely through mime – which is unnerving. Why mascots aren't allowed to talk is one of the questions that mainstream media refuses to tackle and is worthy of a governmental inquiry. Are they not allowed to talk because they know too much? Or because they don't know anything at all? Mascots are creepy. End of.

Decision – Rugby was better in the f'ing old days before creepy mascots appeared

CONCLUSION

There isn't one. And nor should there be. There are aspects of rugby that were better then, and some that are better now. Rugby is and always has been an awesome game and it always will be. Try to enjoy it. Cheers, Paul.

PS: Thanks for reading this book. I genuinely appreciate it.